DEBT and T

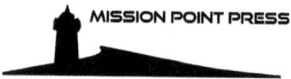

MISSION POINT PRESS

Published by Mission Point Press
2554 Chandler Rd.
Traverse City, MI 49696
(231) 421-9513
www.MissionPointPress.com

ISBN: 978-1-961302-91-4
Library of Congress Control Number: 2024915980

Printed in the United States of America

DEBT and TAXES

DEFUSING AMERICA'S DEBT BOMB

Howard Mick

MISSION POINT PRESS

To my beloved wife, Pat, whose long battle with Parkinson's disease came to an end as this book was being completed.

"Congress shall have Power to lay and collect Taxes… to pay the Debts and provide for the common Defence and general Welfare of the United States…"
— *U.S. Constitution, Article I, Section 8*

"I like to pay taxes. With them, I buy civilization."
— *Oliver Wendell Holmes, Jr., former Supreme Court Justice*

"Everyone in our office pays a higher rate than Warren."
— *Debbie Bosanek, Secretary to Warren Buffett*

TABLE OF CONTENTS

PREFACE

Several years ago, a conservative senator from Oklahoma, Tom Coburn, M.D., wrote a book titled *The Debt Bomb*. His book warned of the dangers to the economy that would be created if the national debt is allowed to grow to a level comparable in size to the gross domestic product. He foresaw a "Debt Bomb" that could explode with dire consequences if not defused. As this book is being written, America has arrived at and surpassed the danger zone identified by Senator Coburn.

Since I am not a well-known author, I thought I would begin by explaining who I am, why I undertook this project and what my methodology has been.

One thing to know about me is that I've been around a long time. I'm in my 90th year of life to be exact. My interest in public affairs goes back to my high school and college years of the 1940s and 1950s when my principal extracurricular activity was debate. I enjoyed the in-depth research required to debate both sides of a subject. That interest has continued throughout my life and may have been a factor in my decision to enroll in law school at the University of Colorado.

I am a first generation college graduate. My father

was a small businessman serving oil field contractors. We moved around a lot in the oil patch. I spent many summers working in the oil fields of Oklahoma, Wyoming and Texas. While in college I enrolled in the ROTC and received a commission in the Army reserves after graduation from law school.

My career choice was to engage in the private practice of law, specializing in corporate and banking law. I began practice in 1959 when the top individual income tax rate was 91% and the top corporate tax rate was 52%. My practice continued for 52 years, during which time there were multiple changes in the tax code.

I was not a tax lawyer per se, but tax considerations were paramount in every transaction I handled for my clients. I was fortunate to work alongside colleagues in my law firm who were among the best tax lawyers to be found anywhere. The daily exposure to transactions with tax implications likely contributed to my ongoing interest in tax policy.

I was motivated to write this book because I agree with Senator Coburn and others who have been alarmed by the growth of the national debt in relation to the size of the economy. In my younger years, politicians, particularly Republicans, were very concerned about the national debt and fiscal policy. Now, we rarely hear mention of the fiscal crisis in the making by any public official. This is concerning to me. My hope is that this book will elevate the level of concern of readers about our fiscal situation and motivate them to urge policy makers in Washington to take action to avert the crisis.

My methodology has been to gather and report facts. I believe in an evidence-based approach to decision-making as opposed to making decisions overly influenced by ideology. The issues covered by this book include the severity of the debt problem today (2024); fiscal history going back to the early post World War II years; policies that resulted in our current situation; the impact that fiscal policy has had on the distribution of wealth and income; reasons why government hasn't done more to arrest the growth in the debt; and what steps can be taken to defuse the "Debt Bomb" before it is too late to avoid dire consequences.

I believe the book makes a persuasive case that the defusing actions I have proposed follow logically from the evidence. But persuading readers to agree with my specific suggestions is not my primary purpose. Mainly, my goal has been to elevate readers' understanding of the causes and seriousness of America's current fiscal imbalance and motivate them to demand that policy makers in Washington place corrective action high on their priority list.

Before proceeding further, I should explain some of the terminology that will appear in the pages that follow:

> **Gross Domestic Product (GDP)** is a monetary measure of the country's total output of goods and services during a specified time period. The term is somewhat more

comprehensive than "national income." There are two ways of measuring GDP growth. "Current dollar" GDP growth includes inflationary growth. "Real" GDP growth is growth after adjusting for inflation. Unless stated otherwise, GDP growth will mean current dollar growth.

Debt, unless otherwise stated, means the indebtedness of the United States government. **Debt Ratio** is the percentage that debt has in relation to GDP. There are two Debt Ratios. The first is the ratio of total Debt to GDP. The other is the ratio of *publicly held* Debt to GDP. The latter ratio excludes Debt held in government accounts, such as the Social Security Trust Fund, but includes Debt held by the Federal Reserve System. The publicly held Debt Ratio is most commonly used by rating agencies and other analysts in measuring a country's financial strength. The term "Debt Ratio" without further specification means the percentage of total debt to GDP.

CBO is the Congressional Budget Office.

INTRODUCTION

By definition, the unsustainable trajectories of deficits and debt that the [Congressional Budget Office] outlines cannot actually happen, because creditors would never be willing to lend to a government [whose] debt, relative to national income, is rising without limit.
Ben Bernanke, former Chairman of the Federal Reserve Board, statement made in 2011.

The dire CBO projections of unrestrained debt growth in relation to national income that Chairman Bernanke was warning about are even more disconcerting in 2024. At the time Chairman Bernanke made that statement, he would have been viewing ten-year CBO projections made in 2010, which forecast the debt held by the public growing to $17 trillion by 2020—approximately 81% of GDP. CBO projections in 2024 predict that debt held by the public will grow to $56 trillion in 2034, 122% of GDP. The CBO further projects a 2034 deficit of $2.9 trillion, of which about $1.7 trillion will be interest cost. We can't let that happen.

Due to variations in tax rates, spending levels, and fluctuations in GDP, one might expect that the Debt

Ratio would rise and fall with the times, with not much change one way or the other. But in this century, we have seen the growth in the debt substantially outpace GDP growth, resulting in an adverse Debt Ratio trajectory. A 23-year adverse trajectory combined with an unprecedented high level of spending to combat the effects of the COVID-19 pandemic have more than doubled the Debt Ratio—from 51% in 2000 to 126% by early 2024. During that same period, the publicly held Debt Ratio increased to just under 100%. The U.S. has sailed past the projections that so concerned Chairman Bernanke 13 years ago. And there is no relief in sight.

The pandemic spending caused the Debt Ratios to reach this stratospheric level in just a few years, but the inevitable result of an adverse trajectory is never-ending growth of debt well beyond the level of GDP. The pandemic just got us to crisis level faster. The remedy is not only to reduce the deficit, but to adjust spending and revenues sufficiently to ensure the growth of the debt is less than the growth in GDP. In other words, ***reverse the debt ratio trajectory.*** When a car is proceeding down a road that leads to a precipice, the solution is not simply to reduce speed. The direction must be reversed. The same applies to the Debt Ratio. The current unsustainable path must be reversed. As depicted on the cover of this book, Uncle Sam needs to stop climbing the mountain of debt where the Debt Bomb awaits and reverse course.

AMERICA'S DEBT RATIO BURDEN IN 2024

Advanced economies like ours that pass 90 percent debt to GDP ratio are less common because they do not survive. Tom A. Coburn, M.D., former senator from Oklahoma, from his 2012 book *The Debt Bomb.*

The late Senator Coburn was an arch fiscal conservative who became known among his colleagues as "Dr. No" because of his opposition to most spending programs. He also believed in limited government and low taxes. But once spending bills were enacted, he advocated paying the bill with higher taxes on the wealthy rather than burdening future generations with debt. He was also a personal friend of President Obama and served on Obama's national commission on Fiscal Responsibility and Reform, also known as the Simpson-Bowles task force.

Senator Coburn was very concerned about the Debt Ratio trajectory that existed more than 11 years ago. In his book, he warned about a "Debt Bomb" that, unless defused, would pass through four stages:

1

Stage 1: Congress tries to maintain the status quo on spending and entitlements.
Stage 2: The United States faces additional ratings downgrades.
Stage 3: Interest rates markedly increase, harming consumers and sending interest payments on the national debt soaring.
Stage 4: Inflation soars and the value of the dollar declines.

As of early 2024, the United States' debt was at about $34 trillion, which is more than 126% of GDP. The publicly held debt had grown to just under $27 trillion, or about $77,000 per capita, $308,000 for a family of four, and nearly 100% of GDP. By the time anyone reads this, the debt burden will have increased.

About 70% of the publicly held debt is held by domestic investors, including Federal Reserve Banks, which hold about $4.5 trillion. The remaining 30% is held by foreign governments and other foreign investors. The non-publicly held debt, amounting to approximately $7 trillion, is held by U.S. governmental accounts, including the Social Security Trust Fund.

The deficit for the fiscal year that ended September 30, 2023, was approximately $2 trillion. That is two thousand billion dollars! Recent projections by the CBO indicate that the 2024 deficit will be $1.9 trillion, nearly the same as 2023. This projection, made in early June 2024, is 27% higher than the projection made in February.

In 2011, the rating agency Standard & Poor's

downgraded U.S. debt from AAA to AA+. On August 1, 2023, the rating agency Fitch also downgraded the rating from AAA to AA+. In explaining the downgrade, the agency published the following statement:

The rating downgrade of the United States reflects the expected fiscal deterioration over the next three years, a high and growing general governmental debt burden and erosion of governance relative to AA and AAA peers over the last two decades that has manifested in repeated debt limit standoffs and last-minute resolutions ... [Tax] cuts and new spending initiatives have contributed to successive debt increases over the last decade.... We expect general government (GG) deficit to rise to 6.3% of GDP in 2023 from 3.7% in 2023, reflecting cyclical weaker revenues, new spending initiatives and a higher interest burden.

The Fitch estimate of the 2023 Debt Ratio turned out to be low. The actual 2023 fiscal year deficit was approximately 7.5% of GDP.

Only one of the three major rating agencies, Moody's, has not downgraded U.S. debt, but has changed its outlook to negative. Here is what Moody's had to say:

The key driver of the outlook change to negative is Moody's assessment that the downside risks to the US fiscal strength have increased and may no longer be offset by the sovereign's unique credit strength. In the context of higher interest rates, without effective fiscal policy measures to reduce government spending or increase revenues, Moody's expects that US fiscal deficits will remain very large, significantly weakening debt affordability. Continued polarization within US Congress raises the risk that successive governments will not be able to reach consensus on a fiscal plan to slow the decline of debt affordability.

It appears that the U.S. has passed through ***Phase 2*** (further rating agency downgrades) predicted by Senator Coburn.

The CBO projects that the interest cost in 2024 will be $893 billion. At that rate, in 2024 the U.S. will pay more than $200 billion in interest to foreign investors. Interest cost will amount to about $12,000 per year per family of four.

The original 2023 estimates of the deficit were surpassed by about $300 billion. Higher interest payments, lower capital gains revenues than in 2022, plus higher than anticipated increases in payments to recipients of Social Security caused by inflation adjustments were major contributors to the increased deficit in 2023.

Multiple sources are expressing alarm about the U.S. Debt Ratio. The International Monetary fund recently expressed concern about America's high level of publicly held debt in relation to GDP. The figure they were looking at was 93% in early 2023. But that is history. As previously stated, the publicly held debt had grown to almost 100% of GDP in early 2024.

There is a strong consensus that high and growing levels of debt will have adverse effects on the economy. The conservative think tank, the Cato Institute, recently issued the following warning:

> *High and growing debt slows economic growth, increases interest rates and crowds out private investment. These negative economic effects will only worsen as the United States' fiscal trajectory deteriorates.*

The World Bank Group recently completed a study to determine at what point sovereign debt as a percentage of GDP impacts real economic growth. The study covered a 40-year period and included more than 100 developed and developing countries. Based on the data reviewed, the authors of the study posited that when the ratio of debt to GDP of a developed economy reaches 77% for an extended period, each point above 77% costs 0.017 percent in real economic growth.

The United States Debt held by the public in early 2024 is about 23 points higher than 77% of GDP. If the study is to be believed, the current Debt Ratio is reducing real economic growth by 0.37% per year. That would reduce real economic growth that otherwise might be at 3% down to 2.63%, a significant drop.

The Debt Ratio is currently too high and is projected

to grow faster than the economy. What do we do if there is another pandemic or other national emergency which requires major governmental outlays?

President Biden's budget for fiscal year 2025 includes forecasts of revenue, spending, and deficits for 2024 through 2025. The forecasted fiscal 2024 deficit was $1.859 trillion, slightly below the revised CBO projection. The numbers are mind boggling. Who would have thought that the U.S. could reduce its annual deficit by $1 trillion and still have a remaining deficit of nearly another trillion. But this "favorable" outcome is subject to variables that are difficult to control.

First is interest rates. The debt is now so large that even small changes in the interest rate have an outsized effect on the deficit. Unexpected demands on the treasury, such as another pandemic, an increase in natural disasters, or an economic downturn are also major risks. An aging population that will create increasing needs for Social Security and Medicare spending presents a continuing funding challenge.

Our fiscal mismanagement during this century has put the U.S. high on the watch list of respected international organizations and rating agencies. Apart from other considerations, we cannot afford to jeopardize our status as the country whose dollar is the world's reserve currency. The United States government should be so financially strong that even a remote discussion of downgrading the rating of our bonds should be unthinkable. The British Pound lost out to the dollar as the major reserve currency. It could happen to us.

U.S. Debt Ratio compared to other countries

In 2024, the *World Population Review* reported that America's Debt Ratio is the ninth highest out of more than 100 reporting countries. The only developed countries that ranked higher were Japan, Italy, Greece, Portugal, and Singapore. (China and Russia were not among the reporting countries.) The U.S. Debt Ratio was attributed to "… high military spending, tax cuts and underfunded programs."

In 2022, Japan's Debt Ratio was an eye-popping 262%, more than double that of the U.S. This naturally raises the question of whether the Debt Ratio is such a big deal: if it is, how does Japan get by? Does Japan's high ratio mean the U.S. has a long way to go before our Debt Ratio becomes a problem? As is often the case, the devil is in the details. A recent study by the Federal Reserve Bank of St. Louis points out the differences between the Japanese governmental accounts and those of the United States.

The level of debt is only one factor that must be considered in gauging the financial position of any business organization or government. Liabilities (debt) is one of three major segments of a government's consolidated balance sheet. The other two are Assets and either Net Assets or Net Liabilities, determined by subtracting Liabilities from Assets. Another consideration is the burden that the country's debt has on the nation's economy.

A major difference between Japan's governmental accounts and those of the U.S. is the Assets account. Japan's governmental Assets account in 2021 totaled

134% of GDP. The U.S. government Assets account totaled 23% of GDP. Japan's largest asset category is their Social Security Trust fund, which in 2021 equaled 55% of GDP. The U.S. Social Security Trust fund is about 10% of GDP. Another difference: unlike the U.S. fund, the Japanese Assets account consists of a diversified portfolio of securities, including more than $1 trillion in U.S. bonds. (Japan is the largest foreign holder, followed closely by China.)

In the case of both countries, when liabilities are deducted from assets, the result is a negative amount. Strangely enough, according to the Federal Reserve Bank, both Japan and the U.S. each had a Net Liability of 119% of GDP in 2021.

But there are other differences which make Japan's debt less burdensome, at least at present. Historically, Japan's debt has been held almost exclusively by domestic investors, including 43% by the Bank of Japan. The percentage held by foreign sources is less than half the percentage of U.S. bonds held by foreign holders. Consequently, in Japan, the interest paid stays largely within the country, while about 30% of interest paid by the U.S. goes to foreign holders.

Another significant difference is the historical spread between the interest paid by the Japanese on their bonds and the return made on investments in their governmental Assets account. Japan's interest costs on their bonds have hovered between zero and 1% for several years. Only recently has the Bank of Japan begun allowing interest on 10-year bonds to exceed 1%. Foreign and domestic debt and equity securities in the assets account have provided a far greater rate of return than Japan's interest cost.

The United States does not enjoy a similar spread between interest paid on debt and yield on investment assets. The yield on the treasury's investment assets is about the same as the rate of interest paid on government debt. Japan's favorable spread makes Japan's Debt Ratio much less burdensome than that of the U.S.

ORIGINS AND HISTORY OF DEBT RATIO GROWTH

We have met the enemy and he is us.
Pogo quote from a 1960s Walt Kelly cartoon.

The Debt Ratio trajectory from 1960 to 2020 in four-year intervals is visualized in the graph below:

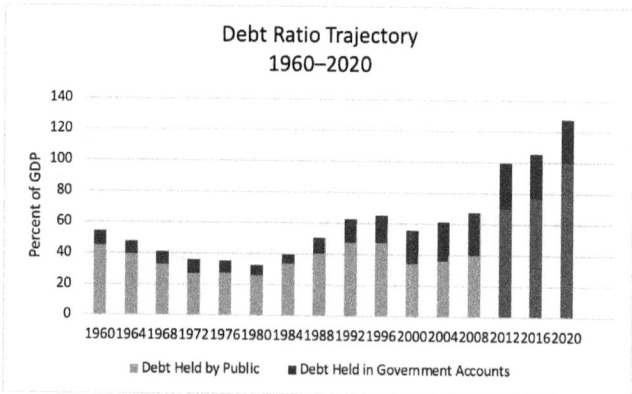

Source: Historical Tables, United States Budget.

Post WW II—1981 Favorable Trajectory

The first year shown in the graph above is 1960, when the Debt Ratio was approximately 55%. If the graph would be extended to the left all the way back to 1946, the bar representing the 1946 Debt Ratio would be at 118%, nearly as high as 2024. The publicly held Debt Ratio, which is not shown on the graph, was 106% in 1946, a record high. The high ratios in 1946 were caused by military spending during World War II and aid to devastated countries in the aftermath of the war.

Between 1946 and 1981, the national debt increased overall because there were more years when there were deficits than when there were surpluses. But in virtually every year, growth in GDP exceeded the growth in the national debt, and the Debt Ratio was brought down from 118% of GDP in 1946 to 31.9% in 1981.

During those post war years, Congress made a conscientious effort to match spending and revenues as closely as possible. Tax increases were not off limits to close any gap. For example, the deficit increased substantially in 1968. As a corrective measure, Congress passed a 10% surtax on all income taxes paid in 1969. The surtax accomplished its intended purpose. Due to increased tax receipts resulting from the surtax, a deficit of $25 billion in 1968 was replaced by a surplus of $3 billion in 1969.

The difference in the attitude of Congress concerning the deficit in 1968 as compared to 2023 is striking. The 1968 deficit equaled 2.8% of GDP—far below GDP growth—but the red ink was of such concern that a surtax was enacted, resulting in a modest surplus the following year.

In 2023, the deficit was 7.5% of GDP, significantly higher than GDP growth, yet the deficit is hardly mentioned in any current political campaign. To create a budget surplus in 2024 through a surtax on income taxes, as was done in 1969, the percentage would need to be nearly 80%, not 10%. This is remarkable when one considers that the budget was in surplus at the beginning of this century.

The post-World War II period can be characterized as one of high taxes and declining wealth concentration. Until 1964, when tax rates were reduced during the Kennedy administration, the top income tax rate was 91%, which applied to incomes over $400,000 per year, the equivalent of $5.1 million in 2024. Wealth concentration, which reached record levels in the late 1920s, was in a state of decline until the 1970s.

High tax rates operated to restrain both pretax and after-tax income. The typical CEO of a publicly held corporation made only about 20 times that of the average worker, far less than the ratio in 2024. In 1968, George Romney, President of American Motors and father of Mitt Romney, turned down large annual bonuses. He remarked that no CEO should earn more than $225,000 per year, more than $2 million in 2023 dollars. The fact that he could have kept only a small portion of the bonuses after tax may also have been a factor.

High taxes were just built into the culture. I remember a joke told by my tax law professor in law school in 1958. The joke was about a wealthy lawyer who prepared a will for a wealthy doctor but declined to send a bill for a $200 fee. Since the doctor would have needed to earn nearly $2,000 to pay the $200 and the lawyer would realize only about $20 after taxes, he suggested that the doctor just send him a bottle of Scotch.

The Kennedy tax cut, which ultimately reduced the top rate to 70%, most likely had a positive effect on economic growth. During the five years following the reduction, GDP growth was significantly higher than in the five preceding years. But the reduction also reduced income tax revenue realized by the government. During the five years preceding the Kennedy cuts, income tax revenue equaled 11.5% of GDP. For the next five years, the average was 10.9%. But due to continuing robust economic growth, the decline in income tax revenue was not sufficient to interrupt the then-prevailing decline in the Debt Ratio trajectory.

Onset of "Starving the Beast" Philosophy

It is a popular belief that the idea of cutting taxes without correspondingly reducing spending originated with Arthur Laffer and his Supply Side economic theory that came to the fore in 1980. But in the late 1970s, the historic emphasis on balancing the budget, championed by conservatives, began to erode. Conservatives were frustrated by what they considered failed attempts to restrain government spending through the regular legislative process, so they decided to advocate a different approach. They reasoned that if the government didn't have the money to spend, Congress could be forced to cut spending. They chose tax cuts as the way to keep money out of the hands of the "big spenders" in Congress. That philosophy became known as "starving the beast," the beast being the government.

Economists such as Milton Friedman promoted this philosophy. In a 1978 article in *Newsweek* he wrote:

> *I have concluded that the only effective way of constraining government spending is by limiting government's explicit tax revenue—just as limited income is the only effective restrain on any individual's or family's spending.*

Economist Irving Kristol wrote in an article in the *Wall Street Journal* that "Tax cuts are essential to shrinking the size of government." He concluded:

> *The politics of the budgetary process is that a cut in any particular program will provoke intense opposition from a minority, and only indifference from a majority. In such a case, it is unreasonable to expect politicians to pay the high political costs involved. They only cut when they are seen to have no alternative.*

Alan Greenspan was also an early advocate of the "starve the beast" philosophy. In 1978 testimony before the Senate Finance Committee, he described his understanding of the purpose of tax cuts:

*Let us remember that the true purpose of any tax cut program in today's environment is to reduce the momentum of expenditure growth by restraining the amount of revenue available and **trust that there is a political limit to deficit spending** [emphasis added].*

Ironically, the first person in government who foresaw the possible development of a "starve the beast" ideology emerging was John Kenneth Galbraith, PhD, a liberal economist who served in the Kennedy administration in the early 1960s.

Dr. Galbraith was concerned that tax cuts adopted in 1963 during the Kennedy administration would register too well with conservatives. In private conversations with President Kennedy, Dr. Galbraith unsuccessfully attempted to dissuade him from supporting the cuts. After leaving the administration, he was free to express his opinion. In testimony before Congress in 1964, Dr. Galbraith stated:

I was never as enthusiastic as many of my fellow economists about the tax reduction of last year. The case for it as an isolated action was undoubtedly good. But there was a greater danger that conservatives, once introduced to the delights of tax reduction, would like it too much. Tax reduction would then become a substitute for increased outlays on urgent social needs. We would have a new and reactionary form of Keynesianism with which to contend.

Dr. Galbraith was correct in foreseeing that conservatives would take such delight in tax cuts that "starving the beast" would become almost universal conservative doctrine. But it took some time. Most Republicans voted against the Kennedy tax cuts in 1964 because the prevailing conservative philosophy emphasized balancing the budget. Two successive Republican presidents, Nixon and Ford, resisted efforts to reduce tax rates, as did former President Eisenhower before them.

But ultimately, the philosophy of "starving the beast" did prevail among most Republicans. Advocates argued that by not only eliminating surpluses but also being willing to accept deficits, government spending could be restrained. Raising taxes to reduce deficits was considered counterproductive, since instead of reducing the deficit, the feeling was that Congress would just increase spending.

The Reagan Years

By 1980, the country was ready for a change in government economic policies, and with good reason. The 1970s has been accurately described as a period of "stagflation." Economic growth was sluggish, and inflation soared, causing Fed Chairman Volker to increase interest rates to nearly 20% in 1981.

During the presidential election campaign of 1980, economist Arthur Laffer introduced an entirely new rationale for tax reduction. He called it Supply Side Economics. Dr. Laffer contended that somewhere between a tax rate of zero and 100% there is an optimum tax rate that allows the government to cover its expenses without overburdening the private sector. This tax rate trajectory was called the "Laffer Curve." The implication was that rates exceeding the optimum might reduce revenues because higher taxes would dampen incentives in the private sector to invest in activities that would grow the economy and increase government tax revenue. The optimum rate was not defined, but apparently it was assumed that the rates in effect in 1980 were too high.

President Reagan acknowledged that his tax cuts would reduce revenue, but as a conservative, he thought Congress was spending too much and that the best way to cause Congress to restrain spending was to reduce the amount of revenue that could be spent. In an address to the nation on February 5, 1981, the former president said:

> *Over the decades we've talked about curtailing government spending so that we can then lower the tax burden. Sometimes we have even taken a run at doing that. But there were always those who told us that taxes couldn't be cut until spending was reduced. Well, you know we can lecture our children about extravagance until we run out of voice and breath. Or we can cure their extravagance by simply reducing their allowance.*

Following President Reagan's election, a major tax reduction was accomplished via the Economic

Recovery Tax Act of 1981. The act essentially in-corporated the provisions of the Kemp-Roth tax bill which cut tax rates across the board by about 25%. The 1981 Act reduced the top individual rate from 70% to 50%. Later, the Tax Reform Act of 1986 fur-ther reduced the top rate to 28% and increased the bottom rate from 11% to 15%. The maximum rate for capital gains was increased from 20% to 28%. There were other provisions designed to make the act revenue neutral despite lowering the maximum rate.

During President Reagan's time in office, economic growth prevented income tax revenues from declining despite the rate reductions. In 1988, the last year of the Reagan Presidency, income tax revenues were $186 billion higher than in 1980. But increased spending, particularly on defense, far exceeded revenue growth, and the national debt grew by $253 billion in 1988. During the Reagan years, the national debt grew from $906 billion to $2.6 trillion, almost triple the 1980 amount, and the Debt Ratio increased by almost two thirds from 31.9% to 50.6% of GDP. In addition to the tax cuts and spending increases, a severe reces-sion early in the Reagan presidency contributed to the growth in the national debt.

But again, income tax revenues did grow despite the tax cuts and the recession. Some advocates of sup-ply side economics will cite the increase in revenues as proof that tax cuts increase revenue. They attribute the deficits to increased spending, not the tax cuts. But the increased spending also increased revenue. By 1988, defense spending was more than double the

1980 amount. This increase obviously created additional jobs and defense industry profits. Those jobs and profits, which were created by government spending, not tax cuts, created additional taxable income and corresponding revenue paid to the treasury.

Conservative economist Bruce Bartlett also points to military spending as one of the engines of growth in the Reagan administration. This is of particular interest because Mr. Bartlett served as a staff member for Congressman Jack Kemp and was the principal author of the Kemp-Roth tax cut bill. He also served as executive director of the Joint Economic Committee of Congress and deputy assistant secretary for economic policy at the U.S. Treasury Department. He held important positions in three Republican administrations: Reagan, Bush Sr., and Bush Jr.

In testimony to Congress in May of 2023, Mr. Bartlett stated:

> *Much of the rise in growth [during the Reagan administration]is attributable to two very important factors ... The first is that Reagan's defense buildup caused government spending for goods and services to go up sharply, thereby increasing aggregate demand.... The second factor which added powerfully to economic growth in the 1980s was the sharp cut in interest rates by the Federal Reserve....*

> **In the end, the Reagan tax cut did not pay for itself. Nor did any administration official or**

> **serious Republican economist make such a
> claim** *[emphasis added].*

Laurence B. Lindsey, a staff member on President Reagan's Council of Economic Advisors and later a Federal Reserve Governor, held a similar view. In commenting on the 1981 tax cuts, he said:

> *The positive economic and behavioral effects
> of the 1981 cuts recouped about a third of the
> revenue losses. Still, it took spending cuts and
> tax increases to move the budget into positive
> territory.*

It may be subject to debate as to whether tax cuts, increased spending, or lower interest rates generated more of the increased revenue during the 1980s. But it is readily determinable that the tax cuts allocated a greater percentage of our GDP away from the treasury and into the bank and investment accounts of income taxpayers than had been the case in previous years. During the Reagan administration, income tax revenues declined from 11.1% of GDP at the beginning of his term to 9.6% at the end.

Although President Reagan advocated tax cuts, he also approved tax increases when he saw the developing deficits. He was not insensitive to the growth in the national debt. The problem was, and continues to be, that tax cuts and opposition to tax increases have been incorporated into standard conservative doctrine.

The "Pledge"

In 1986, at former President Reagan's urging, the "Taxpayer Protection Pledge" (the "Pledge") was created by Grover Norquist, president of Americans for Tax Reform. The Pledge commits politicians who sign never to vote in favor of an increase in income tax rates. By signing the Pledge, an officeholder agrees not only to vote against any proposed tax increases, but also to support reductions in rates to capture any savings generated by eliminating loopholes. Mr. Norquist's stated purpose was, and apparently continues to be, to reduce government down to the size that would "fit in his bathtub." In other words, "starve the beast." In 2023, at least 1400 state and federal politicians had signed the Pledge, including 42 in the senate, 189 in the House, and 18 governors. The Pledge has been signed predominantly, if not exclusively, by Republican politicians, 80% of senators and 85% of Republicans serving in the House of Representatives.

The George H.W. Bush (Bush Sr.) Years

Bush Sr. had the misfortune of inheriting the deficits incurred during the administration of his predecessor. He hoped that the deficits could be controlled without increasing tax rates. In his successful campaign for president in 1988, he made the famous "Read my lips, no new taxes" promise. But after becoming president, he could see that more revenues were needed. Under his watch, taxes were increased, with the top rate going from 28% to 31%. Bush Sr.'s recanting of his "no new taxes" promise likely contributed to losing his bid for reelection to Bill Clinton in 1992.

The Clinton/Gingrich Years

High deficits were still prevailing when President Clinton took office in 1993. To stem the flow of red ink, a Democratic Congress raised taxes again that year, with the top rate increasing to 39.6%. True to their Pledge to Mr. Norquist, not one Republican in Congress voted for the tax increases. Then came 1994.

In 1994, Republicans broke through the 40-year hold that Democrats had on Congress. Newt Gingrich, with his "Contract with America" program, became speaker of the House. From a fiscal perspective at least, an ideal formula may have been implemented. At the beginning of Clinton's term, a Democratic Congress increased taxes. Then, commencing the next year, a Republican Congress likely restrained the growth in spending during the remainder of Clinton's term. With Speaker Gingrich at the helm of the House of Representatives, President Clinton conceded that "the era of big government is over."

Some laws were passed during that period, such as the Roth IRA, that had the effect of reducing tax revenues, but the tax rates established in 1993 were not changed. By the year 2000, a 1992 deficit of $290 billion was converted into a surplus of $236 billion.

The following graph reflects recent history going back to 1977 of government revenues and outlays as percentages of GDP:

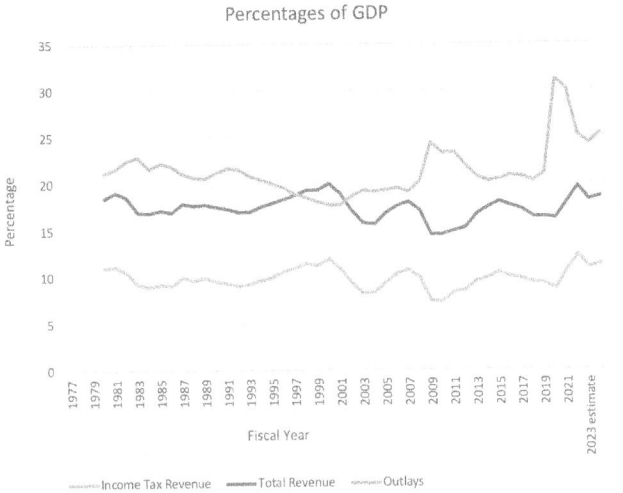

Source: Historical Tables United States Budget, Tables 2.1 and 2.3.

Note that the only time the revenue line crossed over the outlays line, creating a surplus, was during the Clinton/Gingrich years. By the year 2000, income tax revenue had increased to 11.9% of GDP, driving total revenue to 20% of GDP. Spending was reduced to 17.7% of GDP. That year would not have been unusual during the post-World War II period when the Debt Ratio was declining. In those years, annual income tax revenue in the 11% to 12% of GDP range was not unusual. Only in one year in the post-war years prior to 1982 did income tax revenues drop below 10% of GDP. But after 2001, income tax revenues rarely even reached 10%.

The George W. Bush (Bush Jr.) Years

Conservative fiscal policy of "starve the beast" was at its height at the beginning of the 21st century when Bush Jr. was elected. In his 2009 book, *The New American Economy—The Failure of Reaganomics and a New Way Forward,* conservative economist Bruce Bartlett described the prevailing conservative philosophy as follows:

> *Instead of being viewed as the height of fiscal irresponsibility, cutting taxes without any corresponding effort to cut spending was now seen as the epitome of conservative fiscal policy.*

The above philosophy was fully embraced by Bush Jr. He ran on a platform that included tax cuts. He argued that the surplus which existed when he was elected represented an overcharge of American tax-payers. At his urging, in 2001, Congress enacted tax cuts that included reducing the top rate from 39.6% to 35%.

The basic premise of "starve the beast" was that reduced revenue would force a reduction in the size of government. But under Bush Jr., the opposite happened. Spending and the size of government both increased, despite revenue declines First, there was the Iraq war, and later in his presidency, Medicare Part D was adopted. By 2008, a $236 billion surplus had been replaced by a $458 billion deficit. Income tax revenues had declined from 11.9% of GDP to

9.8%. Spending had increased from 17.7% of GDP to 20.2%. The national debt had increased by $4.35 trillion, bringing the total to more than $10 trillion.

The tax cuts and spending increases that occurred during the administration of Bush Jr. persuaded some conservative economists that reducing revenue does not decrease spending, and may, in fact, contribute to spending increases.

William A. Niskanen, PhD, was an economist whose impressive CV included serving as a member and acting chairman of President Reagan's Council of Economic Advisers. From 1985 to 2008 he also served as Chairman of the Cato Institute, a conservative think tank. He earned his doctorate in economics from the University of Chicago.

In the summer of 2007, as Cato's chairman, he authored a report titled, *Limiting Government: "Starve the Beast" Doesn't Work.* In the report, he referred to a study he completed in 2002, which concluded that government spending and revenue after the Reagan tax cuts moved in opposite directions. When revenue increased, as was the case during the Clinton administration, spending declined. When revenue declined, as during the Bush Jr. administration, spending increased. Dr. Niskanen included the following statement in his report, noting that he would like to be proven wrong:

> *One implication of this relation is that a tax increase may be the most effective policy to reduce the relative level of federal spending.*

Dr. Niskanen concluded his report with the following sentence:

> *Reducing tax revenues only shifts part of the burden of government spending to future generations.*

(Dr. Niskanen's report most likely was not favorably received by the Cato Institute or its donors, as he left the Institute in 2008. Bruce Bartlett, who was also once with the Cato Institute, was fired after his first book critical of the Bush Jr. administration was published.)

Dr. Niskanen was not the only conservative economist and Reagan advisor who was alarmed by the failure of "starve the beast" to restrain spending. In the summer of 2007, Bruce Bartlett authored a study titled, *"Starve the Beast" Origins and Development of a Budgetary Metaphor.* In that study, he stated his opinion that until the country is faced with a fiscal crisis, there was little hope that effective steps would be taken to avert it. He said that Americans would start paying attention when deficits reached $1 trillion. (Apparently, he underestimated by at least half.) He observed the following:

> *There is now a growing fear among [some conservative economists] that the ultimate result of relying on starving the beast to support tax cuts may be to make future tax increases inevitable. Whether, on balance, taxpayers*

will be worse off than they would have been without the tax cuts remains to be seen, but there is at least a reasonable chance they will be worse off.

Perhaps a future crisis will provide political cover for massive reductions in entitlement programs that would be politically impossible in the absence of such dire circumstances. However, many analysts now think as I do that the more likely result of such a crisis will be massive tax increases which will bring the tax/GDP ratio in the United States closer to that of Europe.

Again, Mr. Bartlett is a conservative who was actively involved in the creation and implementation of Reaganomics. He wasn't arguing for more revenue to fund new entitlement programs. He was just looking realistically at the popularity of the existing welfare state with Americans and the difficulty of making major reductions in benefit spending, particularly with the impending retirements of baby boomers. This led him to believe that taxes would at some point be substantially increased.

In 2023, sixteen years later, as part of testimony to Congress, Mr. Bartlett submitted a prepared statement which included the following:

By the end of the [Bush Jr.] administration, even Republican economists had little if any-

thing good to say about the Bush tax cuts. Alan Greenspan called for them all to be repealed because their contributions to deficits was greater than their stimulus to growth. The economist Alan Viard of the conservative American Enterprise Institute said in 2011, "The effects of the Bush tax cuts on growth were ambiguous at best. They were not much of a poster child for pro growth policy."

Republican politicians, however, routinely dissemble about the fiscal and economic effects of the Bush tax cuts. As Senator Mitch McConnell said in 2010, long after the handwriting was on the wall, "There's no evidence whatsoever that the Bush tax cuts actually diminished revenue. They increased revenue, because of the vibrancy of these tax cuts in the economy" This was not true. In 2012, the Congressional Budget Office ... concluded that the Bush tax cuts reduced revenue by $3.5 trillion.

The Obama Years

In 2009, incoming president Barack Obama inherited the Great Recession. In that year, income tax receipts plummeted to 7.3% of GDP and continued at low levels for most of Obama's first term. The Bush Jr. tax cuts were still in effect but were set to expire during Obama's term of office. President Obama was reluctant to increase taxes during a recession, and with his support, nearly all the Bush Jr. tax cuts were extended.

Further tax cuts and credits targeted to provide tax relief for families and small businesses were also adopted. The combination of GDP decline, tax cuts, and higher spending caused the Debt Ratio to soar.

In 2011, as the country was emerging from the recession but continued to face deficits, a Democratic Congress increased income tax rates. The top rate was returned to 39.6%. The higher rates and the continuing recovery caused revenues from income taxes to grow to 10.4% of GDP in 2015. The increased income tax revenue helped bring the deficit down to $442 billion, about 2.4% of GDP.

President Obama also tried to corral the ever-growing national debt by appointing a bipartisan task force to make recommendations as to spending reductions and revenue increases. The task force was co-chaired by Alan Simpson, a former Republican senator from Wyoming, and Erskine Bowles, former budget director. Their report was not well received in Congress, as there were spending cuts that were not favored by Democrats and tax increases that were anathema to Republicans. In subsequent years, not only did we fail to see meaningful efforts to inhibit the growth in debt, lax fiscal policies and the COVID-19 pandemic accelerated the growth of the Debt Ratio.

The Trump Years

Donald Trump, the self-proclaimed "King of Debt," was elected in 2016. Running for president he discussed how he would deal with the growth in the national debt:

> *"Nobody knows debt better than me. I've made a fortune using debt and if things don't work out I renegotiate the debt."*

When asked how he would do this as president he said:

> *"You go back and say, 'Guess what, the economy crashed. I'm going to give you back half.'"*

That statement brings to mind a comment attributed to former President Truman:

> *Being dumb is about the worst thing there is when it comes to holding high office.*

The suggestion that America default on its national debt is beyond dumb. Defaulting on the nation's debt is not the same as taking unsuccessful ventures into bankruptcy, which the former president did at least six times. Think of the banks that would be closed and insurance companies that would be unable to pay claims if the value of their government bond portfolio should be cut in half. Think also of the millions of risk-averse private citizens who invested a large part, if not all, of their retirement savings in government bonds. Foreign governments that hold bonds would not be in a forgiving mood. It is already not easy to maintain the dollar as the world reserve currency. It is difficult to imagine the currency of a country that defaults on its obligations retaining that elite status.

But Trump was elected despite losing the popular vote to Hillary Clinton.

In 2017, the Trump administration slashed income tax rates for both corporations and individuals. The cuts dropped the top rate for individuals from 39.6% to 37% and for corporations from 38% to 21%. Other high-end rates were also reduced. The lowest rate was reduced from 15% to 12%, so there was some relief at the bottom of the scale. The estate tax exclusion was increased to $11.4 million and was indexed for inflation. This meant that only married couples with more than $23 million in net assets would be subject to paying any estate tax.

With the national debt totaling $19.5 trillion and the deficit running above $500 billion annually when former President Trump took office, it would not seem to be an appropriate time to cut taxes. But he had no difficulty in putting the tax cuts through. Not surprisingly, income tax revenues declined from 9.9% of GDP when he took office to 9.2% in 2019, a record low in a year of strong economic growth. The decrease in revenue was coupled with increased levels of spending so that the 2019 deficit ballooned to $983 billion.

The following graph compares revenues, outlays, and debt at the beginning of the century with 2019, the last year before the onset of the COVID-19 pandemic, and 2023.

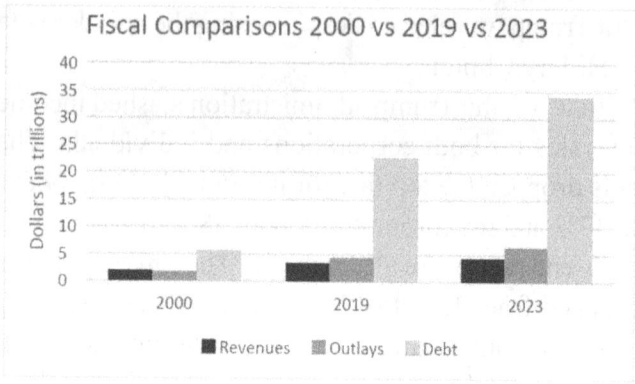

Fiscal Comparisons 2000 vs 2019 vs 2023

Source: Historical Tables, U.S. budget, tables 1.1 and 7.1.

Since Trump not only reduced revenue but increased spending, he did not claim to be starving the beast. Most likely, he was invoking Supply Side theory, because he awarded Arthur Laffer the Presidential Medal of Freedom. In an interview with Sean Hannity of Fox News after the enactment of his tax cut package, Trump declared that by 2021, his tax cuts would cause the national debt to start disappearing "like water."

We saw what happened. The pandemic intervened in 2020, but in 2019, the second year after the tax cuts were adopted, the deficit climbed to nearly $1 trillion and revenues as a percent of GDP plummeted. Even if the pandemic had not occurred, it is difficult to believe that a $983 billion deficit in 2019 would have been converted to a surplus in 2021.

A November 14, 2021, article published by *ProPublica* commented on the Trump deficits as follows:

> *The King of Debt promised to reduce the na-*
> *tional debt—then his tax cuts made it surge.*
> *Add in the pandemic and he oversaw the third*
> *biggest deficit increase of any president [rel-*
> *ative to the size of the economy].... Donald*
> *Trump built a national debt so big even be-*
> *fore the pandemic that it will weigh down the*
> *economy for years.*

Conservative columnist George Will had this to say upon resigning from the Republican party after the Trump tax cuts were enacted:

> *The class interest is to give the people a dol-*
> *lars' worth of government and charge them*
> *80 cents. We used to borrow money for the*
> *future. We fought wars for the future, built*
> *roads, dams, highways, and we borrowed. And*
> *because the future was going to benefit from it,*
> *it was ethical to have them pay part of the cost.*

> *Today we're borrowing to finance our own*
> *consumption of government goods and ser-*
> *vices, which is decadent.*

A comparison of fiscal results between 2000 and 2019 bears out what George Will was saying. In 2000, government revenues totaled 20% of GDP. Spending was 17.7%. 2019, government revenues declined to 16.3% of GDP and as a percentage of GDP, spending increased to 20.9%. A 3.2% increase in spending plus a 3.7% decrease in revenue created a budgetary difference between 2000 and 2019 of 6.9% of GDP, a decline of more than $1.2 trillion in the treasury's receipts vs. outlays that would have prevailed if the 2000 percentages had been maintained.

Of the 3.2% of GDP increase in spending, 2.6% was attributable to increases in Social Security and Medicare spending. About half of the remainder was attributable to increases in defense spending. George Will hit the nail on the head. In 2019, we were borrowing from creditors, including foreign governments and foreign investors, to enable us to pay for 20% of government services and benefits. Rather than having any plan to pay the bill ourselves, we are passing the resulting debt on to future taxpayers. It is decadent.

At a fundraiser held in April 2024, former President Trump declared to his audience, which reportedly included billionaires, that if elected he would extend the Trump tax cuts beyond their expiration in 2025. He included extension of his tax cuts plus additional tax cuts in his governing plan incorporated into the 2024 Republican platform. This would be like pouring gasoline on a fire. The hole is deep enough; we don't need to dig deeper. But much of the country does not see it this way. When a Trump supporter is asked what they like about him, a common reply includes his tax cuts.

An article which appeared in a publication by the Niskanen Center a few years ago may have identified one of the reasons why the cuts are so popular with so many. (The Niskanen Center was established in 2015 in memory of William Niskanen who passed away in

2011.) On May 10, 2017, the center published an article by psychologist Will Wilkinson. The article was titled, "'STARVE THE BEAST' ENABLES BANKRUPT IN CHIEF." Mr. Wilkinson warned about the fallout that would result from the Trump tax cuts:

> *Other than containing less detail, Donald Trump's ... sketch of a "tax plan" is similar to his campaign proposal, which analysts estimate would add $3–5 trillion to the budget deficit.... Republicans often rail against spending, but when the rubber hits the road they reliably increase deficit spending by cutting taxes. This has often been rationalized by the idea that reducing revenue and driving up deficits create pressure to "Starve the Beast" and reduce spending. But big tax cuts create no pressure at all to balance the books. On the contrary, they ease the main pressure that keeps spending and the size of government in check.*

> *[D]ebt offers a way to detach the level of taxation from the level of spending. If you offer voters an opportunity to enjoy lower taxes without corresponding reductions in spending, they'll lap it up. Voters hate taxes and love spending ... [D]ebt-financed spending makes spending feel cheap.*

Debt Ratio Villain: Runaway Spending or Tax Cuts?

An article published by the Center for American Progress on March 27, 2023, concluded that tax cuts played a greater role than spending increases in the deficit buildup. The article states in part:

> *If not for the Bush tax cuts and their extensions—as well as the Trump tax cuts—revenues would be on track to keep pace with spending indefinitely and the debt ratio (debt as a percentage of the economy) would be decreasing. Instead, tax cuts have added $10 trillion to debt since their enactment and are responsible for 57 percent of the increase in the debt since 2001.*

The historical data backs up this conclusion. If income tax revenues had remained above 11% of GDP, as opposed to falling mainly below 10%, the country would have been on a sustainable fiscal path.

To the extent that the negative Debt Ratio is attributable to spending increases, the place to look is entitlements. About 80% of the spending differential between 2000 and 2024 was attributable to increases in entitlement spending. An aging population promises to continue that trend unless reforms are adopted.

As pointed out by Mr. Wilkinson in the article quoted above, Americans love receiving or having their parents receive Social Security benefits and having expensive medical bills covered by Medicare. To the extent that increased spending is responsible for the negative Debt Ratio trajectory, it is due to the government responding to what the voters want. The Trump/Republican platform promises no change in either program. Until the voters focus on the burden that tax cuts and underfunded entitlement spending are placing on future generations, and demand change, nothing will happen.

Those of us who are alive today are the children, grandchildren, and great grandchildren of the "Greatest Generation." Those Americans not only paid high taxes during World War II, but they continued to pay high taxes for decades thereafter to keep the growth in debt well below the growth in the economy. If we don't act to reverse the negative Debt Ratio trajectory prevailing in this century, we could well be known as the greediest (or most irresponsible) generation, passing the burden of debt rather than the blessings of liberty to posterity.

~ III ~

THE PANDEMIC-CAUSED DEBT EXPLOSION

"How did you go bankrupt?" Bill asked. Mike said, "Two Ways: gradually and then suddenly." Dialogue from Ernest Hemingway's novel, *The Sun Also Rises.*

Similar to Mike's journey to bankruptcy, the current national debt crisis resulted from a manageable but accelerating descent, followed by a sudden plunge. From the onset of the 21st century to 2019, the Debt Ratio increased significantly. But then, in 2020, with the arrival of COVID-19, elevated levels of spending brought about an explosion in the debt.

In 2020, the Congress and President Trump responded strongly to assist businesses that were devastated by the pandemic. In that year, government spending exceeded 31% of GDP, a post-World War II record. As will be discussed below, not all of this money was well spent. The deficit in 2020 climbed to more than $3 trillion, an unheard of 14.9% of GDP. Income tax revenues dropped to 8.6% of GDP.

Like former President Obama, President Biden

inherited a crisis not of his making. While the pandemic relief under Trump in 2020 emphasized aid to businesses, under Biden in 2021, relief was directed more to families and the unemployed. The deficit declined only slightly, from $3.1 trillion in 2020 to $2.8 trillion in 2021.

The Aftermath

The $13 trillion in spending and the combined deficits of nearly $6 trillion in just two years have had a profound and continuing effect on the federal budget. The increased debt created by the deficits meant that more revenue would be needed, or borrowing would need to be increased, to pay the interest. The combination of much higher debt and much higher interest rates have been major factors in propelling the Debt Ratio upward on an unsustainable path.

In 2022, the first year after the pandemic, the deficit declined substantially to a reported $1.3 trillion. Income tax revenues climbed to 12.1% of GDP, surpassing even the 11.9% of 2000. Some tax cut advocates cite the 2022 revenue growth as evidence that the Trump tax cuts increased, rather than decreased, revenue. The authors of the recent book, *The Greatest Ponzi Scheme on Earth: How the U.S. Can Avoid Economic Collapse*, make that argument. But let's look at the record.

The Trump tax cuts were enacted in 2017. In four of the six subsequent years, including 2023, income tax revenues were below 10% of GDP. The "Ponzi Scheme" book was published in March 2024. It includes a number of statistics from 2023, but not the decline in income tax revenue that occurred in 2023 or the 2019 deficit of nearly $1 trillion. The authors also attribute the surplus that followed during the Clinton/Gingrich years solely to spending restraint, ignoring the substantial revenue increases caused by tax increases.

The CBO attributed the increased revenues in 2022 to unusually high receipts from capital gains tax receipts stemming from substantial appreciation in stock prices. Unfortunately, a high level of revenues from built-up capital gains cannot be relied on by the treasury as an annually recurring substantial revenue source.

The "Ponzi Scheme" book accurately warns of the threat to our economy created by the adverse Debt Ratio trajectory. The book also makes some thoughtful suggestions with respect to entitlement reform. And it is true that tax increases can be overdone. But the historical record strongly supports the opinions of economists and rating agencies that, contrary to what the Ponzi Scheme book authors argue, tax cuts have been a major factor in creating the current fiscal crisis. The argument that tax cuts increase revenue or even pay for themselves is totally lacking in historical support.

Moving to 2023, the deficit increased to a reported $1.66 trillion. But the reported figures are misleading. The 2022 deficit was inflated due to President Biden's executive order forgiving some student loans. When the loans were written off, the write-off was treated as an expense, resulting in the write-off being added to the 2022 deficit. When the Supreme Court declared the forgiveness unconstitutional in 2023, the loans were restored to the government's books and treated the same as additional revenue. If there had been no write-off and no restoration, which were just bookkeeping entries, the 2022 deficit would have been about $1 trillion and the 2023 deficit would have been $2 trillion.

There were numerous reasons for the large deficit increase in 2023. Revenue declined substantially due to much lower receipts from capital gains taxes. Another factor was that Social Security benefit payments increased dramatically due to an increase in the number of recipients and a large inflation adjustment. Higher interest rates applied to higher debt substantially increased the cost of debt service. Some new spending initiatives were also enacted. With the Trump tax cut rates continuing, income tax revenues declined to 9.7% of GDP, far below the 2022 level.

Two decades of fiscal mismanagement left the country unprepared to absorb the cost of programs adopted to combat the pandemic. A report titled, "Debt to the Penny" issued by the U.S. Treasury, disclosed that as of January 9, 2024, the national debt surpassed $34 trillion, of which nearly $27 trillion was held by the public. This is nearly seven times the debt in 2000 and is an increase of more than $13 trillion since 2019.

Current efforts to rein in the deficit have been feeble at best. The recently enacted Fiscal Responsibility Act (FRA) will have only a minimal effect on projected red ink. The CBO estimated that the FRA will cause the ratio of debt held by the public in 2034 to decline modestly below earlier projections, from 119% of GDP to 115%. This will be a historic high, surpassing even the Debt Ratio during the World War II years and is, no doubt, low due to more recent revised CBO projections.

When trying to come up with a remedial plan for an unsustainable Debt Ratio trajectory, the first step should be to investigate how it might be reduced. This requires looking at the available resources.

~ IV ~

WHERE THE MONEY IS AND ISN'T

For every action in nature there is an equal and opposite reaction. Newton's third law of nature.

The Wealth Concentration Trajectory

The growth in the total national debt to a level exceeding GDP is one of two developments that places the U.S. Debt Ratio closer to that of developing countries than other wealthy countries. The other has been the substantial and disproportionate growth in the wealth of the very wealthiest Americans. Newton's law apparently applies to finances as well. For every reduction in income tax rates, there has been a decrease of funds flowing to the treasury and an increase in the wealth of those who pay the most income tax.

Many Americans are aware that wealth in the U.S. is highly concentrated, but until looking at the data for the purposes of writing this book, I did not realize the extent. According to estimates made by the Federal Reserve Boards, the net assets of the wealthiest 1% of Americans at the end of the third quarter 2023 was more than 60% greater than the publicly held portion of the national debt! That small group had total wealth of $44 trillion, 31% of the nation's total, and dwarfing the $26.9 trillion publicly held debt amount.

For years, I have heard people remark that there is no use taxing the rich because there aren't enough of them. And there aren't that many, relatively speaking. But if $26.9 trillion of the wealth of just 1% of Americans could be converted into cash and transferred to the U.S. Treasury, the publicly held debt could be retired. This 1% would still have combined wealth of nearly $18 trillion, or about 14.7% of the total remaining and about five times the wealth of the bottom 50%. Obviously, this won't happen, nor should it.

Going down the wealth ladder, the wealth of the top 10% in 2023 was $95 trillion, 67% of the nation's total. Not surprisingly, based on the raw numbers cited above, the wealthiest 10% own 93% of all U.S. stocks.

Moving from wealth to income, in the U.S. the top 1% have about 22% of total income; the bottom 50% have about 10%. In Europe, the percentages are nearly reversed. According to a study by *Statista* of seven major European economies, the median for the top 1% was the U.K. with 12.7% of the national income. The median for the bottom 50% was Germany with 18.63%. Of the 38 reporting OECD countries, the United States ranks fifth in the level of income concentration. Only Turkey, Mexico, Bulgaria, and Costa Rica rank higher.

Governmental policies this century have disproportionately benefited the wealthy. More than 70% of the reduced revenue caused by tax cuts accrued to the top 10% of taxpayers. A May 5, 2023, publication by the Institute on Taxation and Public Policy reported from a CBO study that 75% of the reduced capital gains rate and 50% of the pass-through business tax reductions included as part of the Trump tax package went to the top 1%.

The wealthy have by far the largest share of income that can be devoted to savings and investments. Much of the tax-cut money would have been invested in the stock market, farms, real estate, and other investment assets which have experienced almost exponential growth in value over past decades. This has made the additional wealth created by tax cuts worth far more than just the initial amount.

Several years of quantitative easing by the Federal Reserve have been another factor in fueling the concentrated growth of wealth. In his book *The Lords of Easy Money*, *New York Times* reporter Christopher Leonard explains how QE and the Fed's zero interest rate policy flooded the economy with money in search of a return. This phenomenon drove valuations in the stock market and other investment assets ever higher.

Agricultural subsidies have also disproportionately favored the wealthy. According to a Department of Agricultural study, the top 10% of recipients received 79% of subsidies between 2015 and 2021 and the wealthiest 1% received 27%.

Where the Money Isn't

Studies made by the OECD include percentages of workers who have low wage jobs, defined as jobs paying less than two thirds of the median wage. In the United States, 22.7% of the work force held low wage jobs in 2022. This was the fifth highest percentage among the 38 OECD countries. The average was about 15%.

Governmental benefits in the U.S. do not lessen the gap. Other developed countries typically have benefits not found in the U.S., such as universal health coverage and paid maternity leave. A publication of the International Labor organization reports that more than 120 nations have paid maternity leave and health benefits provided by law. The only industrialized nations that do not are Australia, New Zealand, and the United States. The same report states that working women in the United States provide half or more of the income in 55% of households.

Subsidized day care and early childhood education is another area where the U.S. scores near the bottom. In dollar amount spent per child, the U.S. ranks 30th out of 38 OECD countries and as a share of GDP America ranks 34th.

(Perhaps a more generous funding for maternity leave for working mothers and early childhood day care and education would be more effective than abortion bans to reduce the number of abortions, particularly since many women who have abortions are economically stressed and already have families to support.)

A 2020 study by the Rand Corporation disclosed the sharp contrast in income growth from 1975 to 2018. In 1975, the average income of those in the 25th percentile of income was $28,000. If growth had been commensurate with the growth in the economy, their income would be $61,000. The actual was $33,000. In 1975, the average income of the top 1% was $289,000. If growth had been commensurate with the growth in the economy, their income would be $630,000. The actual 2018 average was $1,384,000. The graph below reflects the changes reported in the study.

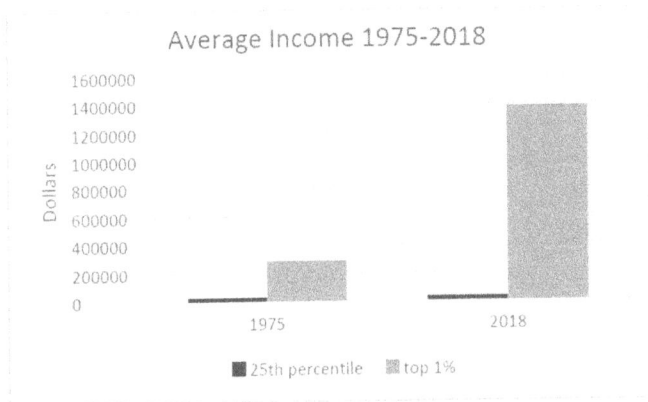

Average Income 1975-2018

A Federal Reserve survey in May of 2023 disclosed that 38% of American adults don't have enough cash to cover a $400 emergency expense. Most of those could find a way to raise $400, perhaps by selling something, borrowing from a relative, or adding it to credit card debt, but a significant percentage could not.

Concentration of income over a long period of years has resulted in an even greater concentration of wealth. A 2023 Federal Reserve report of wealth distribution reveals that in 1989 the top 1% had $4.6 trillion in wealth. The bottom 50% had a combined wealth of about $0.78 trillion. By the end of the first quarter of 2023, the multiple had more than doubled. The top 1% had $43.95 trillion in wealth, while the bottom 50% had $3.44 trillion.

The increase in wealth of the bottom 50% consisted primarily of home values, not financial assets. They could realize a gain on the sale of their homes, but the price of any new home would also have increased. A 2021 study by the American Compass states:

> *With income growth concentrated at the top, middle-income households have not success-fully accumulated savings in recent decades, which also means they have not shared in the gains from rapidly rising asset values. Over the past 30 years, top-quintile households gained nearly $500,000 in liquid net worth on average (after excluding the top 1%), while households in the middle quintile saw their debt rise faster than their financial assets.*
>
> *This is not the widespread prosperity that market capitalism is supposed to generate, and is not the outcome that Americans at any income level should accept.*

Coronavirus Aid, Relief and Economic Security (CARES) Act, and Payroll Protection Plan (PPP) Lending

Grants made pursuant to the CARES Act adopted in 2020 also helped swell the wealth of those already wealthy. Aid to privately owned businesses in 2020 came in the form of loans made under the PPP forgivable loan program. Businesses with fewer than 500 employees could apply for loans through their bank. Companies could then apply for forgiveness of the debt if they could show that they maintained their payrolls at specified levels. A total of $793 billion in loans were made pursuant to the program, and by the end of 2022, $742 billion had been forgiven. The loan forgiveness was not taxable.

It is difficult to understand the thinking of Congress in making forgiveness tax free. What the program did was replace taxable income that recipients might have had, absent the pandemic, with tax-free income. Normally, forgiveness of a loan is treated as taxable income to the debtor. But in this case, the debt forgiveness was explicitly made tax free. The IRS was rebuffed by Congress when the agency attempted to make the forgiveness taxable.

Most of the businesses whose loans were forgiven were so-called pass-through entities. The owners, rather than the business entities, paid tax on the income generated by the business. Losses were also passed through, such that an owner who was active in the business could deduct his or her share of any business losses from his or her outside income.

Here is an example: Assume that in a pre-COVID year a business would typically earn $300,000. But in 2020, due to COVID, earnings declined to $100,000. Let's further assume that the business qualified for a PPP loan in the amount of $350,000 that was forgiven. The forgiveness increased 2020 income to $450,000. The $200,000 decline in taxable income from operations was replaced by $350,000 of tax-free income. Due to the forgiven loan, the total earnings of the business increased to $450,000, but only $100,000 was taxable. The owner had more income but a lower tax bill.

Here is a more extreme example. If instead of declining, the earnings of the business had risen to $400,000, the $350,000 forgiven loan would have swelled the earnings to $750,000 of which $350,00 would have been a tax-free handout by the government.

The PPP loan program was not limited to businesses that needed the relief. The loans were based on employee retention. Consequently, virtually any business with fewer than 500 employees qualified for the loan and forgiveness, subject to the level of employee retention.

The assumption in passing the legislation was that only companies that needed relief would apply. But businesses are owned by human beings. It is human nature not to turn down government handouts. When a business owner sees others accepting the largesse, he or she will very likely be happy to join in.

With no requirement of need, one of the companies that applied for a loan was the Los Angeles Lakers. They received a $4.6 million loan. There was such a backlash that the funds were returned. But a business owned by Tom Brady received a loan of just under $1 million that was reportedly forgiven.

As is often the case with government handouts, it is the wealthy who have the resources and know-how to jump to the head of the line. A study by the Federal Reserve Bank of St. Louis found that only one quarter of the loans operated to save jobs that would otherwise have disappeared, and the loan benefits flowed disproportionately to wealthy households. Mr. Leonard reported in this book that:

> *[M]ore than half of the PPP money went to just 5% of the companies ... Fully 25% of all PPP money went to 1% of the companies. An analysis by the Federal Reserve and others found that the PPP money saved about 2.3 million jobs at a cost of $286,000 per job, after President Trump claimed it would save or support 50 million jobs.... About $651 billion of the CARES Act was in the form of tax breaks for businesses which were complicated to obtain. This meant that the tax benefits went largely to the big companies that could hire the best tax lawyers.*

The program was also plagued with fraudulent claims. In a report dated June 27, 2023, the Inspector General's office of the Small Business Administration estimated that due to the rush to disburse the funds, approximately $200 billion —17%—of PPP loans were disbursed to fraudsters.

Since need for assistance was not a criterion for receiving PPP forgiven loans, the program was in large part a program of subsidies for privately owned businesses. No doubt it helped many to weather through the pandemic, but the program was not carefully drawn to minimize amounts going to companies that had no need for help or to avoid windfalls resulting from converting, or adding to, taxable income by making debt forgiveness tax free.

Large publicly held businesses also shared in the largesse. The airline industry received relief totaling $54 billion, about half of which was grants and half was low interest loans.

One airline, American Airlines (AA), received $4 billion in outright grants and $1.7 billion in loans. AA needed the bailout in part because during the preceding five years, AA had repurchased more than $11.9 billion in stock. This included $1.2 billion repurchased in 2019, funded in part by the Trump corporate tax rate cut. As part of the overall package negotiated by Treasury Secretary Mnuchin, the government received warrants to purchase AA stock amounting to less than 1% of the total outstanding.

What a deal! After a $4 billion grant, which equals about 40% of AA's 2024 market cap, and a $1.7 billion low interest loan, still more money will be required for the treasury to acquire less than 1% of AA's stock. One would think that at least 10% or 15% of the AA stock would have been issued outright to the treasury for the $4 billion grant. In that event, the value of the AA stock held by others would be diluted by 10% or 15%, but the purpose of the bailout was to preserve jobs and an industry, not stock market values.

Other airlines received similar deals. The airline bailouts were needed to save an important industry and associated jobs, but the terms were decidedly one-sided, benefiting affluent shareholders. The terms contrast sharply with the auto industry bailout a dozen years ago when the government received 61% of GM's common stock plus preferred stock.

In her book *The War on Small Business,* economist Carol Roth concludes:

> *When the federal government stepped in with the "assistance" via the Coronavirus Aid, Relief and Economic Security (CARES) Act, it clearly favored the big, wealthy, and well connected.*

In a July 8, 2022, article titled, "Federal Reserve Economists Have Harsh Assessment of the Government's Small Business Relief Program," columnist Jon Miltimore wrote:

> *Federal Reserve data show US households added $13.5 trillion in wealth in 2020, largely from "stimulus" spending that flooded the system with money.*

> *The new wealth was not evenly distributed. Nearly $10 trillion of it went to households in the top quintile.*

Considering all the data that was included in the preceding paragraphs, it would be understandable if a reader were to conclude that the author is anti-wealth.

Not true. The above discussion is not a criticism of the wealthy, but of some of the government policies that had the effect of inflating wealth without commensurate benefits to the overall general welfare. As an attorney in private practice specializing in corporate and banking law, a very high percentage of my clients were among or close to the top 1%. By and large, the wealthy are the entrepreneurs who have built businesses and created employment opportunities; many share their wealth via major philanthropic support; they donate not only money but their time and talents to support the greater good. The free market is one of America's best characteristics; it enables entrepreneurs and others who develop talents employed for the benefit of the community to be rewarded financially. But the devil is always in the details. The pendulum has swung sharply in the direction of wealth concentration. The farther it keeps going in that direction, the more extreme the reversal in direction will likely be. Leftist revolutions generally occur after the pendulum in the affected country has swung too far to the right.

Each dollar spent by the government is a tax on somebody. Since the pressure to balance the budget disappeared, Congress has been unable to come up with any suitable guideline to relate spending to revenue. The easy route has been to spend regardless of the debt and pass the bill for our spending on to future generations. Those who have benefited the most are those who otherwise would have paid more of the bill—the wealthy. If the U.S. is to reverse the Debt Ratio trajectory, which it must, the resources held by wealthy must come into play as a major part of the solution.

~ V ~

OBSTACLES

When you find yourself in a hole, stop digging.
Will Rogers, American humorist.

Making abrupt changes in government policies is like trying to turn an ocean liner around on a dime. Creating awareness of the reality of exploding national debt, let alone taking effective remedial action, will be difficult. Americans are accustomed to thinking of the national debt as a problem which will affect tomorrow, not today. Notwithstanding the warnings from respected sources over many years about the threat posed by the rapidly ascending Debt Ratio, it will likely take some time before the runaway national debt receives the attention it should. Polarization in Washington makes the problem worse. Acting in the near term to reverse the debt ratio trajectory is not on anyone's to-do list. The pressure must come from voters who understand the problem and demand action.

As compared to past years, the political parties have moved in opposite directions away from the center. The term "Moderate Republican" has virtually become an oxymoron. Low taxes and limited government have replaced balanced budgets as accepted conservative dogma. The Blue Dog Democrats, who are probably the most fiscally conservative caucus in Congress, have been decimated in number, declining from 54 members at their high to 10 in 2023.

A majority of Democrats view other perceived needs as higher priorities for any revenue increases than reversing the trajectory of the Debt Ratio. It is difficult to advocate tax increases to meet perceived social needs and at the same time advocate for spending cuts and more tax increases to reverse the trajectory.

Republican Pledge signers are just as beholden to the Pledge and the creator, Grover Norquist, as ever. According to one report, before voting on the deficit reduction package recently passed by the House, Republican leaders wanted to be sure that certain provisions did not constitute a tax increase. They sought advice from Grover Norquist as to whether voting for the bill would violate the Pledge.

Mr. Norquist gave his approval but suggested that GOP leaders provide him with a written promise not to allow a tax increase to be included in any deficit reduction bill. As reported in a May 3, 2023, article by Paul M. Krawzak, GOP leaders provided this assurance in the form of an exchange of letters between Ways and Means chairman, Jason Smith, R-MO, and then-Speaker Kevin McCarthy.

Congressional Republicans are continuing to follow a "starve the beast" strategy, initiated by conservative economists and a much-admired president more than 40 years ago. But by 2007, some of these same economists, including Dr. Niskanen and Mr. Bartlett, who helped draft the legislation implementing the policy, realized it wasn't working and was only passing much of the bill for our spending on to future generations.

Unfortunately, instead of paying attention to the advice of those economists and allowing evidence to inform their actions, conservatives in government took the political route, hitching their star to Grover Norquist via the Pledge. While an ounce of prevention could have held the problem at bay, the U.S. now requires more than a pound of cure. And the longer it takes for signers of the Pledge to renounce the Pledge and be willing to exercise all powers granted by the Constitution, including the power to increase taxes, the longer it will be before any meaningful remedial actions to address the pending fiscal crisis can be considered. Meanwhile, the pound of cure becomes heavier with each passing year.

In his book, *The New American Economy—The Failure of Reaganomics and a New Way Forward,* published in 2009 at the onset of the Great Recession, Bruce Bartlett summarized the problem:

> *I believe that when this second fiscal crisis hits sometime in the next few years, it is inevitable that higher revenues will be needed to plug much of the fiscal hole. Unfortunately, both parties are in denial about this. Republicans still delude themselves that tax cuts*

starve the beast and that tax increases feed it, while Democrats are so afraid of being seen as tax increasers that they simply refuse to acknowledge reality. Obama's proposed tax increases were all carefully packaged with tax cuts in order to counter the charge he was a tax increaser.

When the crunch comes and the need for a major increase in revenue becomes overwhelming, I expect that Republicans will refuse to participate in the process. If Democrats have to raise taxes with no bipartisan support, they will have no choice but to cater to the demands of their most liberal wing. This will mean higher rates on businesses and entrepreneurs, and soak-the-rich policies that would make Franklin D. Roosevelt blush.

In 15 years, nothing has changed. The situational analysis made by Mr. Bartlett in 2009 is a perfect description of the political landscape in 2024. I recommend his book to anyone who wishes to deepen their knowledge of fiscal history and learn what a conservative economist who was part of the Reagan team has to say about possible solutions.

The Pledge and Limited Government vs. the Constitution

The "Pledge" and the underlying "Starve the Beast" ideology must be based on the assumption that there is nothing that the government can spend money on that is worth the tax to pay for it. The typical Pledge signer must subscribe to the view that the founders favored limited government. Consequently, driving the size of government down by refusing to increase taxes to pay for legislated expenditures serves a higher purpose.

But the founders did not agree on the role of government. George Washington and Alexander Hamilton favored a robust national government with implied power to take actions expressly granted by the Constitution. Thomas Jefferson envisioned an agrarian country with decentralized government.

In truth, we don't know what the views of the founders would be today. Most probably they would disagree just as our current leaders today have disagreements. But as a guide, they clearly stated in the preamble what the purposes of government are:

> ... to form a more perfect Union, establish justice, insure domestic tranquility, provide for the common defense, promote the general Welfare and secure the Blessings of Liberty to ourselves and our posterity ...

Further, Article I, Section 8 provides:

> Congress shall have Power to lay and collect taxes ... to pay the Debts and provide for the common Defense and general Welfare of the United States ...

And what could serve a more "Constitutional" purpose than raising taxes to pay debts as provided in Article I, Section 8?

The founders left it to future generations to determine what actions and policies should be followed to provide for the common defense and promote the "general Welfare" in their generation. Needless to say, the founders' generation was far different from ours. In 1790, approximately 90% of the labor force worked on farms. A typical farm would be as small as 10 acres, sufficient to feed a family. The population was just under four million. It would have taken extraordinary vision for them to have known what actions government should be taking when the population has grown to 335 million and only about two percent live on farms.

Competing Ten-Year Budget Plans

President Biden's long-term fiscal plan is incorporated in his fiscal 2025 budget proposal. Spending increases and additional taxes on the wealthy and large corporations are included in the budget. He proposes to achieve deficit reduction of $3 trillion over ten years by measures such as a 25% minimum tax on billionaires; eliminating deductions for executive compensation in excess of $1 million paid by C corporations; increasing the corporate tax rate and strengthening the ability of the IRS to crack down on wealthy tax cheats. Some middle-class tax reductions offset part of the revenue gains from tax increases targeted at the wealthy.

But deficits over that period in the president's budget are projected to average more than $1.5 trillion annually, ballooning the debt to $42 trillion by 2034. In his budget, the publicly held Debt Ratio in 2034 is projected to increase to 105%. Assuming the U.S. can find lenders fo finance a $42 trillion debt, a 4% interest means an interest expense of more than $1.6 trillion. We need to do better.

The GOP-controlled Congress has devised a deficit reduction plan which Republicans contend will result in a small surplus in 10 years. The plan would limit 2024 discretionary spending to the 2022 levels and then limit discretionary spending increases to 1% over a ten-year period. Other reductions would be made by tightening work requirements for Medicaid support and food stamps. Payment to states and reimbursements to hospitals would also be cut. No increases in tax rates are included. Instead, Republicans argue that increased revenue can be realized through economic growth, which they believe can be enhanced in part by more tax cuts. They contend that the cuts will help increase GDP growth to 3% per annum, adding $3 trillion in revenue that can be applied to deficit reduction. The plan says very little about entitlement spending other than recommending that a bipartisan commission be appointed to suggest reforms.

These competing proposals are evidence of the truth of what economist Bruce Bartlett predicted 15 years ago. The Democrats are frightened to death of being viewed as tax increasers. President Biden's budget does not propose increasing taxes on anyone making less than $400,000. This would mean that the Trump tax cuts would not be allowed to expire in their entirety, as rates on incomes below the $400,000 level would be increased. Instead of shared sacrifice, only the top 3% or 4% of taxpayers would be called upon to pay more taxes. Since the average income of those in the top 5% is about $335,000, not even everyone in the top 5% would be asked to pay more. It seems obvious that any workable solution will require reaching farther down, at least including all taxpayers at the top 5% and 10% levels.

Turning our attention to the Republican plan, as Mr. Bartlett prophesied, the Republicans continue to be addicted to forcing the size of government down by depriving it of tax revenues. But we also see evidence that some still cling to the fantasy that tax cuts increase revenue.

According to the Center for Budget and Policy Priorities, the Republican plan would require an 8% reduction in discretionary spending below 2023 levels. If spending for defense and veterans' benefits, which constitute more than half of discretionary spending, were simply excluded, which is likely to occur, other programs would need to be cut 23%. Moreover, according to the center, many of the programs are already feeling the effects of the 2011 Budget Control Act. In other words, the cuts most likely are politically and operationally impossible without substantial cuts to veterans' benefits and defense spending.

Going back to 2019, if there had been no discretionary spending other than for defense, the treasury would still have been required to borrow 6% of the budget.

There will likely also be future demands for additional spending. Global warming is happening. Spending for disaster relief is likely to increase as well as spending to mitigate the effects of rising sea levels and salinization of water sources. The U.S. is still behind other developed countries in infrastructure spending. A *Statista* report ranked the U.S. 32nd out of 37 selected countries in the share of GDP dedicated to infrastructure spending. The leading country was China, with more than nine times the level of the U.S. In the future, more, not less, spending on infrastructure will likely be required.

The suggestion that tax cuts stimulate sufficient GDP growth such that the resulting revenue reduces the deficit is not supported by historical evidence. Going all the way back to 1963, the beneficial effects of tax cuts have consistently been offset by a reduction in the share of GDP realized by the government via income tax revenues. Additional tax cuts might be a stimulus, but they will have a net negative effect on the Debt Ratio.

Finally, the plan asks nothing or next to nothing of those who have benefited from government tax and other policies over the past decades and have the greatest capacity to help reverse the Debt Ratio trajectory. Instead, the plan shifts the burden to the states, hospitals, and those who are dependent on Medicaid and food stamps to have sufficient nutrition and health care.

Both plans do little more than kick the can down the road. (A more accurate analogy might be rolling the snowball down the mountain, gaining size and momentum with each rotation.)

At a conference held in January of 2024, Karen Dynan, the former chief economist at the Treasury Department and a senior fellow at the Peterson Institute for International Economics, said the following:

> *I don't think that lawmakers are doing us a service by declaring some fixes off the table. President Biden has promised not to raise taxes on people earning less than $400,000 per year and Republicans are determined to extend tax cuts for people earning even above that. I've argued that higher taxes have to be part of the budget fix.*

The Democratic Obama administration appointed a bipartisan task force to suggest a plan to stem the flow of red ink. Perhaps with the political cover of voter demands, a future Democratic administration could be persuaded to take similar action.

Based on the newly released Republican platform, there would appear to be little hope that revenue increases and entitlement reform will be considered. According to the CBO, just extending the Trump tax cuts will add $4.6 trillion to the national debt by 2034. President Trump has also raised the possibility of additional tax cuts. As to entitlement reform, the Trump/Republican platform promises to make no changes to Medicare or Social Security.

We cannot predict what the future will bring. Ten-year projections don't seem to ever work out, particularly the optimistic ones. Stuff happens. Let's not leave dealing with the problems our generation has created to future generations. Past generations have taken bold action to make our life better. As our gift to posterity, why not take some bold action now to better prepare the country for whatever may lie ahead?

The country needs a higher degree of awareness of the Debt Ratio trajectory that leaders such as Chairman Bernanke and Senator Coburn warned about when the problem was much less severe. Once we as a country focus on the problem, we will realize that failure to reverse the trajectory is not an option, and that the sooner we address the problem soberly and in a bipartisan fashion, the better off we will be.

All options must be on the table. Pledge signers must realize that the Constitution is the only governing document to which they will adhere and tell Mr. Norquist that the Pledge needs to be set aside. Liberals need to be willing to place some of their priorities on hold until we get the fiscal mess straightened out.

An independent bipartisan task force may be our only hope to restore fiscal sanity to proceedings in Washington. Task forces for this purpose have been organized in the past and they have done good work, but unfortunately, their recommendations have not been followed. The divisions are such that only strong urging by voters and an administration that is open to the idea will result in such a task force being formed.

Returning to a balanced budget discipline in the near future is likely not feasible. A substitute goal could be limiting the growth in the Debt to an amount less than the growth in the economy, In the next two chapters, I suggest a two-step approach that could reverse the Debt Ratio trajectory and place the country on a much stronger fiscal path going forward.

STEP 1: REDUCE THE DEBT

My friends and I have been coddled long enough
by a billionaire-friendly Congress. It's time for our
government to get serious about shared sacrifice.
Warren Buffett quote from 2011 op-ed
in the *New York Times*.

The data reported in Chapter IV could support the argument that since tax cuts and many other government policies have favored the wealthy it would be fair to ask them to bear the lion's share of the cost of remediation. But in times of national need, fairness is secondary to averting a crisis. If there is an attack on the country by a foreign power, the young and strong must be called on to respond by risking their lives in the military. Some people are just born at the wrong time and reach military age when a war is raging. Is it fair? No, but it is necessary. If the problem is the need to reduce debt and reverse an adverse Debt Ratio trajectory, the solution must be to look where the money is. The data clearly shows that there is not much room for those in the bottom 80% to have benefits cut or taxes increased. But what is the best approach?

In 2010, Senator Pete Domenici, Republican from New Mexico, and Alice Rivlin, a former budget director in the Treasury Department, co-chaired a task force that proposed a deficit reduction plan to bring the debt-to-GDP ratio down from a projected 70% at the end of 2010 to 52% by 2030. The Rivlin-Domenici task force report did not propose reducing the national debt. Instead, it focused on bringing the annual deficits down to a level below the growth in GDP (reversing the Debt Ratio).

In 2012, the task force published a supplemental report titled, *Domenici-Rivlin Debt Reduction Task Force Plan 2.0.* At about the same time, a task force headed by former Wyoming senator Alan Simpson and former White House chief of staff Erskine Bowles, issued their plan. The Domenici-Rivlin supplemental report included the following statement:

> *As we released our report, the National Commission on Fiscal Responsibility and Reform, led by former Senator Alan Simpson and former White House Chief of Staff Erskine Bowles also delivered their plan.*

> *These bipartisan plans came to similar conclusions: First, the present debt trajectory of the federal government cannot be sustained and poses grave dangers to the American economy; second, our policy makers must make*

> *difficult decisions to get our fiscal house in*
> *order; and third, any realistic solutions must*
> *contain structural reforms to entitlements and*
> *fundamental tax reform that raises significant*
> *new revenue.*

As with other attempts to bring about meaningful action to control the debt, the efforts of the two task forces yielded little in the way of deficit reduction.

The Domenici-Rivlin approach, which did not include paying down the debt, may have been sufficient to reverse the trajectory in 2010 when the national debt was 90% of GDP and the debt held by the public was 60%. But in early 2024, the Debt Ratios have soared past those levels to 126% and almost 100%, respectively.

To quantify the deficit reduction required to reverse the Debt Ratio trajectory, it is necessary to make a realistic estimate of current dollar GDP growth. The CBO has projected that in 2024, the current dollar growth will be 4.8%, 2.0% real growth and 2.8% inflationary growth. That is below the average for this century. Consequently, a reasonable assumption going forward could be current dollar GDP growth of 4.5%. Applying that percentage to 2024 GDP of about $27 trillion results in projected growth of $1.2 trillion.

Based on the 2024 projected deficit of $1.9 trillion to bring the deficit down to $1.2 trillion, the deficit would need to be reduced by $700 billion. But that would only stabilize the ratio. With 4.5% current dollar GDP growth, to reverse the Debt Ratio, deficit reduction of more than $700 billion would be necessary.

High interest rates are compounding the difficulty of the problem. Interest on the national debt for 2024 is projected to be $893 billion. This is based on an average interest rate of 3.22%. But as bonds mature, they are being replaced by bonds bearing higher rates of interest. Each increase of 1% in the average interest being paid on the national debt would increase the deficit by $310 billion. And that is based on the debt level in early 2024. The trend isn't good: higher interest rates being applied to growing debt.

In October 6, 2023, the *New York Times* reported that the government was paying average interest of 4.7% per annum on newly issued debt. The *Times* also reported a shrinking pool of foreign buyers who are in the market for purchasing U.S. debt. It is basic economics that more supply and limited demand lead to higher interest costs. Officials at the Federal Reserve Board meeting in September of 2023 predicted that interest rates could remain high for years to come.

If the country should decide to take action to reverse the Debt Ratio, which unfortunately is not currently on the horizon, there would be two potentially workable choices.

- Forge ahead with revenue increases and spending reductions with the economy being weighed down by interest payments on the national debt; growing from $893 billion to more than $1 trillion in just a few years.
- Pay the debt down by a feasible amount

to reduce the interest burden, lowering the amount of deficit reduction that must be funded by increased taxes and spending reductions.

Debt Ratio Variables

The variables which determine the direction of the Debt Ratio trajectory are listed below:

- **GDP growth**
- **Interest rate paid on the debt**
- **Tax rates and sources of revenue**
- **Government spending**
- **Debt amount**

The debt amount is a variable that has a direct effect on all of the others. The obvious reasons are:

- **A large debt burden inhibits growth in GDP** as interest costs absorb resources that might be used more productively in the private sector or invested in infrastructure or other programs that would enhance growth. (Note the previously discussed study that quantified the decline in GDP growth when publicly held debt exceeds 77% of GDP.)
- **High debt puts pressure on interest rates** by increasing the supply of debt to be financed by a limited demand pool of investors.

In early July of 2024, when it appeared likely that Donald Trump would be elected President, the July 6–12 issue of *The Economist* noted:

Yields on ten-year Treasuries have risen as investors contemplate a Republican sweep in November which would make deficit-financed tax cuts more likely.

- **High debt requires more revenue to pay the interest,** thus requiring the government to increase tax rates and/or identify other sources of revenue.
- **Higher debt necessarily increases government spending** due to increasing interest cost on a large principal.

Each of the above factors should place paying down the debt high on the priority list of all of us, particularly conservatives. High debt has a negative effect on at least two components of private wealth:

- High interest rates drive down the value of investments;
- High interest rates slow the economy and put pressure on earnings of stocks held as investment assets.

By participating in the reduction of the debt, those doing so could well be shoring up the value of their remaining investments.

The United States is still a wealthy country, with a national net worth more than five times the amount of the publicly held national debt. The better off among us have the ability to make a significant pay-down of the debt enough to take the country out of crisis territory without breaking a sweat. With a lower debt level, the task of reversing the Debt Ratio trajectory would become less daunting. Consequently, the ideal plan would be one which has an initial step of making a significant up-front reduction.

Although income in the U.S. is highly concentrated, with the top 1% having about 21% of the total income, wealth is even more concentrated. The top 1% have approximately 31% of total wealth in the U.S. Many pay very little or no income tax. An early May 2024 guest essay in the *New York Times* stated that in 2018, the average tax paid by the 400 wealthiest Americans had declined to 23%, down from 56% in 1960. The same article reported that the bottom half of wage earners paid 24% of their income in taxes.

This leads to the question of whether a tax on wealth should be considered as a means of paying down the debt. Just such a proposal was made in 1999 by none other than Donald Trump when he was considering running for president on a third party ticket. He proposed a wealth tax of 14.5% on Americans having a net worth of $10 million or more. The tax would have raised over $5 trillion, sufficient at that time to retire the national debt. Subsequently he stated that he no longer supports the proposal, preferring to advocate tax cuts as reflected in recent statements and in the Trump/Republican platform.

President Trump's 1999 proposal would have retired the debt. My suggestion would only bring the debt down to about $26.5 trillion, a reduction from 126% of GDP to 100%, still too high, but markedly better than the level that prevails as this book is written. A one-time tax to reduce the debt would be unprecedented, but the fact that a president once proposed a similar tax lends support to my argument that a pay-down is not just a theoretical possibility but is feasible and not strictly out of left field.

With a few exceptions such as Switzerland, Norway, and Spain, most experiments with wealth taxes by other countries have not been successful. (France and Spain no longer have a tax on net wealth but levy a tax on certain assets.) But in fairness to other taxpayers, if there is to be a major reduction in the debt, all wealthy citizens, not just those who pay income tax, should participate.

A single-year wealth tax targeted to raise $7 trillion could enable the government to reduce the debt held by the public to about 73% of GDP. The tax could be graduated so that a small percentage might be applied to those at the lower ranges of wealth, and a higher rate on those at the very top. This reduction would bring the Debt Ratio down to about where it was when Senator Coburn published his book warning about the "Debt Bomb."

But there could be a question whether an outright wealth tax is constitutional. Section 2 Article 9 of the Constitution mandates that all direct taxes laid be "… in Proportion to the Census or Enumeration…." There could be a risk that the current Supreme Court would find a wealth tax unconstitutional since it would not be apportioned based on population. (The 16th Amendment authorizing Congress to levy a tax on incomes was adopted to clarify that income taxes are not subject to the limitations of Article 1, Section 9.)

Congress might be able to cause a wealth tax equivalent to fit clearly within Constitutional restraints by including unrealized gain as income for the purpose of this tax. The tax might be measured by wealth, but the tax would only be assessed against current income and unrealized gains. Constitutionality could then depend on the degree of deference the Court would give to Congress in defining income.

Recognizing that many of those who would be subject to the tax don't have sufficient cash lying around to pay all at once, payment could be spread over a period of up to three years with interest at the rate of 3-year treasuries on the unpaid portion. The debt reduction would not be immediate as to the deferred portion, but the interest received would reduce the net interest paid by the treasury.

Payments out of IRA accounts and private foundations might be permitted to facilitate raising the amount needed. Investments held in private foundation would not be counted as wealth for purposes of the tax, but the primary donor would have the option of using funds from the foundation to satisfy his or her tax liability.

That brings up questions of how a debt reduction tax might be structured and how it would impact wealth concentration. The Federal Reserve Board recently published a table showing how wealth growth between 1989 and the first quarter of 2023 accrued to those in different strata of wealth. I have added a column that shows what the distributive effect of a $7 trillion debt reduction tax would be if the tax is allocated substantially as stated in the table:

| 1989 | | 2023 | | After Tax |
Wealth %	Wealth %	Wealth %	Tax $	Wealth %
Top .01%	8.7%	12.8%	$2.52T	11.6%
Next .99%	14.2%	18.5%	$2.27T	17.8%
Next 9%	37%	37.7%	$2.21T	38%
Next 40%	36.3%	28.6%	$-0-	30%
Bottom 50%	3.8%	2.4%	$-0-	2.6%
Total	100%	100%	$7T	100%

Note that from 1989 to 2023 the top 1% (top two categories in the table) saw their share of total wealth grow from 22.9% to 31.3%, an increase of nearly 37%. The share of the next 9% changed very little while the share of wealth of the bottom 90% experienced significant declines. As shown in the above table, even after giving effect to the one-time $7 trillion tax, the top 1% in the U.S. would still have a much higher share of total wealth than they had in 1989.

In terms of dollars, the top 1% (the top two categories in the table) would see their wealth combined reduced from $43.95 trillion to $37.15 trillion.

Individual tax allocations on wealth might look something like the following:

Under $1,000,000: no tax
Next $2,000,000: 3%
Next $2,000,000: 4%

Next $5,000,000: 10%
Next $40,000,000: 12%
Above $50,000,000: 16%

To reduce the impact of the tax, those paying the tax might be allowed a credit against their estate tax liability. Lower rates and longer payouts might be provided for illiquid assets, including interests in privately owned businesses.

The one-time tax could strengthen the economy by reducing the national debt and the attendant interest costs. This could help shore up the value of the remaining wealth of those who pay the tax. Hopefully they might conclude that it is better to surrender a portion of their wealth to reduce the national debt than incur losses in market value because of an economy weighed down by a huge national debt.

Recently, a group of at least 260 millionaires and billionaires wrote a letter demanding that taxes on the wealthy be increased to help remediate worldwide income and wealth disparity. The letter was directed to global leaders gathered at the World Economic Forum in Davos, Switzerland.

The proposed tax to raise the amount I suggested would not have much of an effect on wealth concentration, but it would have the important effect of reducing the country's debt burden. Many wealthy are motivated to use their wealth to support charitable causes. It would be difficult to identify a charitable donation that would be more beneficial to the U.S. and its people than paying down the national debt. It could also help save the reputation of our generation which, if the Debt Ratio trajectory is not reversed, could well be remembered as the generation that squandered the legacy of the "Greatest Generation" through greed, political polarization, rigid adherence to failed ideologies and incompetence.

It could also be beneficial to include large corporations in this one-time effort. The Trump 2017 tax cuts reduced the corporate tax rate from 38% to 21%. Since the 2017 tax cuts, corporations have increased their stock buybacks by more than 50% compared to levels prior to the tax cut. Buybacks averaged nearly $900 billion per year during the 2021–2023 period. A temporary surtax designed to raise $900 billion from large corporations, payable over a period of up to three years if necessary, could simply cause them to forgo a year or so of buybacks to help dig the country out of a hole. The tax might combine a temporary surtax on income and a tax on average buybacks over the most recent three years.

Rather than paying down the debt with all of the additional revenue from the corporate surtax, half or so might be added to the Social Security trust fund. This would extend the life of the fund and enable the trustees to begin a program of diversifying the investments. Perhaps publicly held corporations that meet investment standards established in advance could pay part of their tax by issuing shares of stock to the Social Security Trust Fund. (See discussion below regarding the fund's current investment restrictions.)

Paying down the debt would be an important first

step in reversing the Debt Ratio. The $7 plus trillion reduction in the national debt would reduce the annual interest burden by $300 billion, or close to it, and over a 10-year period, counting interest savings and savings of interest on interest, the debt would be reduced by more than $11 trillion. This one-time payment would not reverse the Debt Ratio trajectory, but the immediate deficit reduction resulting from the lower interest cost would make the task far less daunting.

If the wealth tax doesn't gain traction, an alternative could be a temporary deficit reduction surtax on high income taxpayers The surtax would be assessed for a specified period of time to raise a targeted amount. This alternative would not likely raise as much as the wealth tax proposed, but any amount would reduce the amount of deficit reduction that would need to be effected by tax increases and/or spending cuts.

With the debt still being so high after the pay-down, the wild card will continue to be interest rates. There is also no way to predict what unexpected crises might arise that require more spending. The pay-down alone will not solve the problem. But the country will be in a far better position with it than if we continue with the burden of a $34 trillion and growing debt dragging on the economy. Regardless of how we do it, what is certain is that we need to get started.

~ VII ~

STEP 2: REVERSE THE DEBT RATIO TRAJECTORY

*We don't mind paying taxes at Berkshire … The federal government owns a percentage of the earnings of the business we make … and they can change the percentage any year…*Warren Buffett

It bears repeating that continuing with a trajectory of debt growth surpassing GDP growth is not an option. Continuation will lead to one or both of the conclusions posited by former Fed Chairman Bernanke and former Senator Coburn. At some point, absent reversal, creditors will cease being willing to finance our debt, as suggested by Chairman Bernanke, and/ or we will reach the state of hyperinflation and de-valuation of the dollar described by Senator Coburn.

In chapter VI, I suggested that reversal of the Debt Ratio could likely be achieved by reducing the deficit to 4.5% of GDP, or approximately $700 billion. The full pay-down of $7 trillion through the wealth tax and $450 billion from the one-time corporate tax would likely save more than $300 billion in interest cost.

Realizing the $400 billion balance of the needed deficit reduction would not be a slam dunk but it would be much less difficult than dealing with the full $700 billion. The allocation between increases in revenue and reductions in spending will need to be determined by negotiation, assuming the policy makers can be induced to start the process.

In negotiating a path forward, progressives, as well as true fiscal conservatives, such as the late Senator Coburn, should have a seat at the table. Those conservatives may not agree with some of the spending, but passing the bill on to future taxpayers is more distasteful to them than increasing taxes to pay for it. There is nothing in the Constitution about Grover Norquist's bathtub. Either the Pledge must go or those who insist on adhering to it must be marginalized. Tax increases, not cuts, must be a major part of the deficit reduction formula.

In comparison with other developed countries, the U.S. is a low tax country. In 2022, U.S. state and federal tax revenues totaled 26.6% of GDP. According to a study made by the OECD, this was the lowest of any developed country. The average in 2021 was 34.5%. Much of the difference is attributable to funding higher levels of public benefits provided by other developed countries which more than offset the greater military spending by the U.S. Ironically, perhaps, polls indicate that the populations of the Scandinavian countries such as Finland, Denmark, and Sweden are the happiest. As reported in the study mentioned above, taxes in all of those countries exceed 40% of GDP.

I am not sufficiently conversant with all the ways the government spends money to suggest specific cuts in discretionary spending. No doubt there are some that should be made. Part of the task of a bipartisan task force would be identifying where funds might be wasted through inefficiencies or lack of need. This would be an important step that the government owes to taxpayers. Hopefully, by focusing on spending with a critical eye, savings can be found and a lean, stream-lined, and effective government can emerge.

But as previously mentioned, there are also needs that will require more spending to satisfy. More flight controllers are needed. Additional personnel and better pay may be necessary to assure air safety. The U.S. has a much higher child poverty rate than nearly all developed countries. Too many poor children are not kindergarten-ready and never catch up. The U.S. ranks 32nd out of 37 OECD countries in public spending for early childhood education as a percent of GDP and 30th in the dollar amount spent per child.

Infrastructure spending, although recently in-creased, is still far short of the amount needed to meet requests for infrastructure projects and repairs of crumbling bridges. Increased spending to combat the effects of climate change, including more frequent and severe storms, will almost certainly be required.

The IRS needs more funding. Cheating on taxes is every bit as much of a crime as shoplifting or burglary. Failure to fund the IRS sufficiently to create a credible concern among taxpayers that their returns might be audited is like failure to fund the police.

With outdated computer systems and staff shortages, the IRS can barely administer its office. I accidentally overpaid my 2022 income taxes by a significant amount. My refund was delayed a total of five months as I kept receiving form letters from the IRS saying they needed more time, including one such letter sent after the refund had already been made. My accountant told me not to bother calling them because they wouldn't answer the phone. When I did receive my refund, I was pleased to receive interest at the rate of 5%, money the IRS could have saved if the agency had been able to act more promptly. Fortunately, a recent increase in the service's budget has alleviated some of the problem.

No one likes higher taxes, but our situation will not improve with time. And with combined federal, state, and local revenue of about 26.6% of GDP, compared to an average of 34% among all OECD countries, there is room for increases.

Raising the Revenue

Allowing the Trump tax cuts to expire on schedule in 2025, possibly retaining the reduction at the lowest level of income, would be a good start. But other taxes will also be needed. Adding a new rate of 45% for incomes above $2 Million, 50% for incomes above $10 million and 60% for incomes above $20 million could make sense. Raising income taxes by 1.5% of GDP would raise $400 billion. That would bring income tax revenue up to 11.3% of GDP, still below the 11.9% of 2001.

Allowing three-year income averaging would enable those who have a one-year bulge in their income to avoid the high rates designed for those with continuing high income.

Corporate rate adjustments *might* need to be increased to 30% plus 5% on income applied to stock repurchases.

A value added tax (VAT) should also be on the table. The United States is the only developed country that does not have a VAT. Rates range from a low of 5% in countries such as Canada to an average of 21% in Europe. A VAT tax is on consumption, so in that respect it is regressive. But if combined with helping to fund benefits for lower income households, and as a substitute for higher rates at lower income levels, there could be a place for a VAT. Structurally, it is more efficient and less noticeable to taxpayers than income tax.

Following are some other possible taxes to increase revenue:

- Enact a transaction tax on trades on stock exchanges.
- Increase the gas tax, which hasn't been raised since 1993.
- Remove the favorable treatment for qualified dividends in excess of $50,000 per year.
- Tax capital gains above $500,000 at ordinary income tax rates.
- Make so-called "Cadillac" health insurance plans taxable.
- Decrease the estate tax exemption back to $5

million, and increase the top rate to 50% for estates over $20 million and 65% for estates over $100 million, allowing for deferred pay-outs with interest.

- Eliminate favorable capital gains treatment for so-called carried interests.
- Treat borrowings against appreciated stock values as a sale of the stock.
- Levy a capital gains tax on appreciated assets held at death. (Currently, extremely wealthy individuals minimize their tax liability by a strategy known as buy, borrow and die. They buy assets that appreciate in value, borrow to pay for them and then avoid a tax on the gain by holding them until they pass away so that their heirs receive a stepped up basis tax free.)

The above suggestions are made from a high-level perspective. A more detailed analysis and negotiation will determine what adjustments are made. If our representatives in Washington can be persuaded of the necessity of reversing the Debt Ratio trajectory as soon as possible, and put all options on the table, a negotiated solution is possible.

There will be those who argue that tax increases of the magnitude suggested will have a negative effect on the economy. They have a point, but spending cuts will also have a negative effect. We can all live better today if we can pass the bill on to future taxpayers. But we are now at the point where in addition to the unfairness of passing the bill on to future taxpayers, the interest cost which results from this practice is having a negative impact on the economy and will only worsen the longer we wait.

Some conservative analysts and organizations have argued that income tax rates should not be increased because the tax is already progressive. Typically, the top 1%, with about 22% of the income pay a little more than 42% of income taxes. (Due to the large amount of capital gains revenue in 2022, the percentages were 26.3% and 45.8%, respectively.) They argue that deficit reductions should be implemented almost entirely on spending cuts, including entitlement spending. If additional revenues are needed, they argue that the government should look to a consumption tax or other broadly based revenue increase.

But what are our alternatives? If the concentration of wealth and income were closer to those of the U.S. in 1975 or Europe today, then a broad-based tax would make more sense. But, as already pointed out, the financial resources of the U.S. are not broadly shared. A recent article in *The Hill* notes that:

> Of all income above the poverty level in America, nearly one third is flowing to the top 1%. That's extreme inequality.

The bottom 50% have very little capacity to absorb tax increases. Significantly higher taxes and/or reduced benefits affecting that group would not only create hardship, but would reduce their capacity to spend. Their decreased spending would also damage the economy.

Taxes should be assessed where they will have the least adverse effect on the "general Welfare." People whose incomes are barely enough to get by should not be called upon to pay significantly more in income tax or new taxes. They pay other taxes, and as stated above, a higher share of their income than the richest 400.

Historically, those with the most income have paid a disproportionate share of the income tax. In 1928, those with incomes of $50,000 or more paid 78% of the income tax. Income of $50,000 per year in 1928 would be the equivalent in 2023 of more than $800,000, well into top 1% territory. Income taxes, as well as estate taxes, have always been paid primarily by the affluent.

We can take some comfort in the fact that the U.S. has had years of good economic growth when the taxes were much higher. After the Kennedy tax cuts in the mid 1960s, when the share of income of the very wealthy was less than half what it is today, the top rate was 70% on incomes over $200,000. That would be the equivalent of $2.087 million in 2024. The corporate income tax rate was also far above any proposed amount today, 52% on income above the equivalent of $255,000. Yet the economy experienced vigorous growth. The same was true after the Clinton tax increases.

Arthur Laffer may be correct in his assertion that taxes can be so high that they discourage entrepreneurship and result in lowering revenue. But the Laffer curve also acknowledges that taxes can be too low to pay the costs of government. And that has been the multiyear reality of U.S. government finances.

No business or government can operate solely by rigid adherence to ideology. Walmart's business model emphasizes low prices, but if they refused to increase prices when necessary to offset increases in costs the company would not have survived. We might favor low taxes and small government, but taxes must be sufficient to fund the government we have, not the one we might like to have. If we want to reduce the size of government, it should be done via the legislative process, not by driving the country into bankruptcy. To achieve near-term reversal of the adverse Debt Ratio trajectory, more revenue, as well as spending restraint, will be needed.

~ VIII ~

AGING POPULATION CHALLENGE

Social Security is not the hard one to solve. Medicare, that is the gorilla in the room, and you've got to put all of it on the table. President Joe Biden.

Underfunded entitlement programs have been major contributors to the negative Debt Ratio trajectory. The separate trajectory of an aging population will increasingly place demands on the two major programs serving the elderly, Social Security and Medicare. By 2030, all baby boomers will have reached age 65. Nearly one out of every five Americans will be 65 or older. The older baby boomers will be approaching 85 years of age. Although the U.S. has fallen behind other developed countries in extending life expectancy, medical care has improved over the years, and retiring baby boomers will as a group live longer than previous generations.

Social Security
Social Security has been a lifeline for many senior and disabled Americans for 90 years. Benefits are

funded by payments from payroll tax revenues and from a reserve account referred to as the Social Security Trust Fund. From 1939 to 1983, all benefits were paid through the trust fund. In 1983, when additions to the trust fund became insufficient to pay legislated benefits, Congress adopted amendments which included increasing the FICA tax sufficiently to create a surplus in the fund.

Annual surpluses from 1984 to 2021 resulted in the trust fund growing to $2.9 trillion. But the surpluses have been dissipated by increased demand. At the time of this writing, the Trust Fund is running at a deficit which is projected to exhaust the fund in 2034.

By law, all moneys in the trust fund must be invested in United States government obligations. When the Social Security Act was adopted in 1934, the country was in the midst of a depression and was suffering the effects of a stock market crash. It was understandable that Congress limited investments to U.S. government securities. Similarly, when amendments were adopted in 1983, the stagflation of the 1970s and the poor returns on the stock market were fresh in the minds of Congress. High rates were also continuing to be paid on government bonds. The law requiring the trust fund to be invested solely in U.S. government obligations was not changed.

In later years, some thoughtful writers questioned the wisdom of creating a trust fund for American workers that was restricted to investing in government securities. In 1999, a commentary by Robert D. Reischauer in a Brookings Institute publication argued that the limitation shortchanged American workers. He surmised that Congress never acted to revise the policy due to concerns about possible political pressure on investment decisions. Mr. Reischauer argued that problems such as political pressure could have been prevented by requiring the Trust Fund trustees to appoint independent investment managers.

A less restrictive investment policy would have had at least three major benefits. First, the balance of $2.9 trillion in the trust fund in 2021 would likely have at least doubled. The value of the stocks in the S&P 500 in 2000 had more than quadrupled by 2023. If a conservative policy of investing 40% to 45% in stocks had been included in the portfolio, a doubling in value could have easily occurred. Instead of worrying now about making Social Security solvent for the long term, the treasury could be paying a far greater percentage of benefits from the Trust Fund. Instead of needing to increase payroll taxes, it might have been possible to reduce them. If trustees of a private or charitable trust had invested funds held in trust solely in government bonds over an extended period, they could likely be sued for mismanagement.

The second benefit is that to the extent that funds would have been invested in securities other than those issued by the United States government, there would have been an alternate source of payment for benefits. Whether the government makes payments directly from taxes, or from paying off bonds in the Trust Fund, beneficiaries now have no place to look but the government for the payment of benefits.

The third benefit would have been to prevent the funds being treated no differently from any other source of revenue. Politicians of both parties disregarded the borrowings from the Social Security Trust fund in reporting annual deficits. The borrowings were added to the national debt, but not counted in the annual deficits which were more publicized. Until the surpluses stopped growing, we simply had a regressive payroll tax as part of the overall financing of government spending. This meant that less reliance had to be placed on income taxpayers. Essentially, receipts from a regressive payroll tax replaced receipts from a progressive income tax that resulted from tax cuts.

Actions such as the following could help restore the financial soundness of the Social Security payment system:

- Remove the individual income limit on payroll tax payments to subject all earned income to the tax, not just those below the limit.
- Charge a higher income tax rate, such as 50% on benefits paid to beneficiaries who have outside income of $200,000 or more. All or part of this tax would be returned to the trust fund.
- Supplement the fund through the one-time tax mentioned in Chapter VI.
- Begin the process of diversifying the investments in the trust fund so that perhaps within five years and thereafter, as much as half would be invested in equities and fixed income securities other than U.S. government

bonds. The goal would be to create a perpetual fund similar to a university endowment fund. A larger, more diversified fund, enhanced by the $500 billion tax proceeds mentioned above, would have a better chance of outlasting the surge of benefits to be paid to retired baby boomers.

- Increase the age to receive full benefits to 69.
- Replace inflation adjustment by limiting payment increases to beneficiaries to the lesser of inflation or the percentage of average wage increases. This would limit benefit growth to the growth in income of those paying the benefits.

A Republican study group of which Speaker of the House Johnson is a member, has proposed various limitations on Social Security and Medicare programs, including increasing retirement age for Social Security benefits. No tax increases are included. I'm not suggesting that the Republican plan necessarily be adopted, but at least parts should be considered in bipartisan negotiations. This proposal was made before the Trump/Republican platform promising no changes was released.

Medicare

Healthcare reform is long overdue in the United States. The amount that the U.S spends on health care is double the average amount per capita that other developed countries spend. The argument that government programs are inherently less efficient than those in the private sector does not hold up in the healthcare sector. Administrative costs absorb about 17% of healthcare spending with private insurance. Medicare administrative costs are about 2% of spending. Those figures may exaggerate the true difference. Medicare patients are older and more likely to have illnesses that are more expensive to treat. This would bring down the percentage of administrative costs per dollar spent, but the difference is still undoubtedly substantial.

Overall, U.S. administrative costs are estimated to be about 8.3% of total health care costs according to a CAP 20 study. The study listed 13 other high-income countries. The median for those countries was 3%. The low was Norway with 0.6% in administrative costs. Since other rich countries tend to have single-payer systems, the comparison lends support to the conclusion that single payer systems can be more efficient than the U.S. system of private for-profit insurance.

There is somewhat of an unfair aspect to employer-provided insurance which is common in the United States. While we think of employers as paying the cost of the insurance, we actually have a consumer-financed system. The ultimate payers are those who purchase the products or services provided by employers who have plans for employees. Like all expenses, health care insurance costs are built into a company's pricing decisions. Low-income consumers whose employers either do not provide insurance or who cannot afford the portion required to be paid by employees are helping to pay the healthcare costs of others. Fortunately, the percent of uninsured Americans has been declining, and in 2022 stood at 7.9%, a substantial number, but only about half the number that existed before enactment of the Affordable Care Act.

If we are looking for a system for the U.S. to emulate, we might consider the system adopted in Switzerland. In Switzerland, every resident is required by law to purchase basic health insurance from one of 50 not-for-profit insurance companies approved by the federal government. Although the federal government sets the basic requirements of the policies and evaluates the cost-effectiveness of the system, general administration is diffused among the cantons.

Under the Swiss system, premiums paid can vary based primarily on the deductible chosen. Lower income residents receive subsidies to assist them in paying the premiums. Those wanting a wider range of choice in choosing physicians and hospitals can purchase supplemental insurance.

Beyond stating the obvious—that Medicare needs to be placed on a cost-sustaining basis through expense reductions and increased revenues—I claim no expertise or even above average knowledge about all the complex issues involved in setting up and administering a cost-effective healthcare system. That is a task for those who are much better informed. But creating a more cost-effective and inclusive system, like dealing with the national debt, should be a national priority.

~ IX ~
GROWING THE ECONOMY THROUGH IMMIGRATION REFORM

The bosom of America is open to receive not only the Opulent and respected Stranger, but the oppressed and persecuted of all Nations and Religions; whom we shall welcome to a participation of all our rights and privileges. George Washington.

Increased tax revenue and targeted spending reductions alone will not reverse the Debt Ratio. A strong and growing economy is equally or more important. The obvious reason is that the Debt Ratio is a measure of GDP growth versus Debt growth. Immigration reform may the low hanging fruit in our efforts to enhance GDP growth. Our broken immigration system must be fixed.

Robust economic growth will require more entrepreneurs and a growing labor force of skilled and unskilled workers. Historically, immigrants and second-generation Americans have been some of our most successful entrepreneurs and are an important source for workers. According to the Immigration

Learning Center, 25% of new businesses are founded by immigrants. This ratio is more than double their share of the U.S. population. Immigrants also have a higher rate of participation in the workforce than citizens born in the U.S. There are about 44 million immigrants in the United States. More than half are U.S. citizens. A large percentage of the others are documented.

In July of 2022, I attended a seminar on inflation at the Aspen Institute in Colorado. The panel consisted of Laurence Fink, founder and CEO of Blackrock, the largest money management firm in the world, economist and former Treasury Secretary Lawrence Summers, and Neel Kashkari, the President of the Federal Reserve Bank of Minneapolis. A *Wall Street Journal* financial reporter acted as moderator.

Mr. Kashkari emphasized that the Fed would continue to raise interest rates until inflation is reduced to 2%. When asked why 2% was the target, he replied it is because that is what the Federal Reserve Board had established. Any changes would damage their credibility.

Dr. Summers did not disagree with the actions the Fed was taking, but his view was that the interest rate increases were more likely than not to cause a recession. He also commented that the general population's mistrust for the "Elite" was a major stumbling block to progress, because due to their education and experience, they are best equipped to help chart a path forward.

Mr. Fink opined that inflation is a policy problem. He said the country needed to admit many more immigrants to join the workforce to help relieve inflationary pressures. He stated that labor shortages are a major factor in creating the inflationary environment.

Of the three panelists, only Mr. Fink's suggestion would contribute to economic growth as well as restrain inflation. Two factors affecting GDP are the number of workers and worker productivity. Immigrants are among our most productive workers.

Approximately 10,000 baby boomers are retiring every day. Rather than contributing to GDP growth as workers, as retirees they will create a need to increase Social Security and Medicare spending, resulting in a negative influence on the Debt Ratio. More workers are needed to fund those benefits.

Immigration reform that enables the country to secure its borders while accepting at least two million immigrants per year should be a no-brainer. We have jobs that are not filled—two million in the hospitality industry alone. Healthcare workers are also in short supply, and the situation will worsen with the aging baby boomers. While two million per year may sound like a lot of immigrants, given the total U.S. population and economy, two million immigrants could be absorbed with barely a ripple.

The entrepreneurs and professionals in this country very often are immigrants or children of immigrants. Two of the physicians I see are of Arab descent and two are of Asian descent. I recently had an X-ray of my knee. The technician was from Ethiopia. My wife is in a skilled nursing facility. Four Kenyans and a Filipino provide her with high quality nursing and related services. Members of our family have a small company and recently hired a Kenyan immigrant to a management position.

Immigrant entrepreneurs and highly skilled professionals help create good jobs. Overall, they don't take them away from those who are already here. Apart from contributing to GDP growth, a well-conceived and executed immigration plan hits the sweet spot in meeting other needs and solving problems. By combating inflation, immigration growth could lead to lower interest rates. A larger workforce would also increase the number of workers paying payroll taxes to pay benefits to Social Security benefit recipients.

Although the recent surge in illegal immigration will require a vigorous enforcement program, including some deportations, rounding up and deporting millions of undocumented immigrants who are already here, as advocated by President Trump, would be massively counterproductive. Following are some estimates published in the May 15, 2024, issue of the *Washington Post,* citing a 2019 study by the Migration Policy Institute:

- A third of undocumented immigrants were from places other than Mexico and Central America, including Asia.
- A fifth had been in the country for more than 20 years and about 60% had resided in the U.S. more than 10 years.
- A third had children who are U.S. citizens.
- Two thirds—6.8 million—were employed.
- Three in ten owned homes.

It would be difficult to conceive of a more impractical, expensive, unwise, economically damaging, and cruel action than rounding up and deporting millions of U.S. residents. What do we do about their homes, or their children who are U.S. citizens? How can we justify making a family choose whether to leave their citizen children behind or take them to a foreign, potentially not English-speaking or unsafe country?

"Dreamers" is the term used to refer to immigrants who arrived in the U.S. as children in 2007 or earlier. For a time, they were protected from deportation under the Deferred Action for Childhood Arrivals executive order (DACA) adopted by President Obama. DACA was cancelled by President Trump, reinstated by President Biden, and then struck down by the Supreme Court. A study published in January 2022 by the George W. Bush Presidential Library stated the following about the Dreamers:

> *Many Dreamers know only the United States as home, only speak English and have their own American families…. Without the contribution of Dreamers … the United States would lose $460.3 billion in GDP over the next decade and remove 685,000 workers from the economy.*

Deporting them would not only disrupt their lives, but would be like shooting ourselves in the foot. We need their contribution to our economy and national well-being.

Immigration policy cannot be based on emotional anecdotal incidents of crimes being committed by undocumented immigrants, or on unfounded claims that other countries are emptying their jails and mental institutions to send undesirables to America. Studies indicate that immigrants, including undocumented immigrants, are less likely to be incarcerated or arrested than native Americans.

And immigration policy is not just about border security, although that is important. The policy should be based on the contributions immigrants make to a vibrant growing economy, not on racism or concern about how immigrants might vote.

~ X ~

SUMMARY AND CONCLUSION

Ask not what your country can do for you, but what you can do for your country. Former President John F. Kennedy.

We associate the term "inconvenient truth" with Al Gore, who used the term to describe global warming and its potential effects. Although the overwhelming number of scientists worldwide recognize and have warned about the problem, and we are already seeing the effects, there continue to be some who are in denial. Others might agree that there is global warming, but not about the causes.

But there can be no dispute about America's growing adverse Debt Ratio. It is recorded in black and white in government records. In just 24 years, the national Debt has increased by a factor of six and the Debt Ratio has more than doubled. Governmental budget projections, which make little or no allowance for unforeseen extraordinary demands, foresee Debt growth in perpetuity amounting to $56 trillion by 2034.

It does not require an advanced degree in economics to understand that the adverse Debt Ratio cannot continue indefinitely. Major deficit reduction needs to take place. Based on historical data, I have suggested that reducing the deficit to 4.5% of GDP, or about $700 billion, would offer a reasonable opportunity to reverse the Debt Ratio trajectory. I have also suggested that reducing the amount of the debt through a wealth tax equivalent would be feasible and immediately reduce interest cost, facilitating the $700 billion deficit reduction. With less debt to finance, the pay-down might also create an opportunity for the treasury to borrow at lower rates.

But reducing the deficit by $700 billion per year is still possible without the pay-down, just more difficult. Any positive action is better than inaction and much better than actions that would worsen the situation.

The fiscal plan included in the 2024 Trump/Republican platform would greatly exacerbate the pending Debt Ratio crisis. The plan would extend the Trump tax cuts, legislate more tax reductions, leave Medicare and Social Security untouched and "Carry out the largest deportation operation in American history." If we were in search of a plan to accelerate and make more certain the consequences that would flow from detonation of the "Debt Bomb," it would be difficult to improve on what is contained in that platform. But about all that can be said for the Democrats is that they have not signed pledges to resist taking one of the actions which must be part of any workable plan to reverse the Debt Ratio: increasing taxes.

America has almost always responded to a challenge once it is identified. The Debt Ratio will be reversed because there is no other choice. The questions are when and how.

As to the "when," as daunting as beginning the task today may seem, it is very unlikely that reversal will ever be easier. To the contrary, reversal will become even more difficult with each year the adverse ratio continues and the debt grows faster than GDP.

The overall components of the "how" have been obvious for several years. Task forces from a dozen years ago, led by four very smart people—Former Senator Alan Simpson and Erskine Bowles heading up one task force, and former Senator Pete Domenici and Alice Rivlin heading up the other—said it loud and clear:

> *... any realistic solution must contain structural reform with entitlements and fundamental tax reform that raises significant new revenue.*

The data in the preceding pages back up what these task forces were saying. Tax cuts and refusal to consider tax increases have been major contributors to the problem. Tax increases along with spending reform, particularly with respect to entitlements, are indispensable ingredients of a successful solution.

Unfortunately, there is no sign that policy makers in Washington will awaken any time soon to the need for bipartisan action. The impetus must come from the voters. One thing we can do for our country is to demand that our representatives in Washington take prompt action to resolve our pending debt crisis. There is no other option. Appointment of a bipartisan task force to consider all possible means of deficit reduction is a must. Pray that in spite of all the obstacles, it happens soon.

A Post-Election Addendum begins on page 118.

ENDNOTES

The quotes appearing in this book were found by a Google search entering the name of the person and the word "quotes," ("Eisenhower quotes") or by the quote. Much of the statistical data has been taken from the Historical Tables included each year in the Federal budget documents: *www.whitehouse.gov/omb/budget/historical-tables.* References to table numbers in these notes refer to the tables in the Historical Tables. Tax rates quoted at various times in the book were taken from the tables published by the Tax Foundation, which can be accessed through a Google search for "historical tax rates."

Nearly all the research for this book was done via a Google search of keywords. When an article or source was found, the web address was often so lengthy that all of it did not appear in the search. Consequently, I have often referenced the source by using the key words I used to access the source, rather than the web address. For brevity, I have placed the key words I used in parentheses preceded by the letter "G" if a Google search.

Introduction

Page xiii *Chairman Bernanke would have been viewing....* The Budget and Economic Outlook Fiscal Years 2010 to 2020 (CBO) (G-CBO debt projections 2010–2020).

CBO projections in 2024.... The Budget and Economic Outlook 2024-2034 (CBO) (G-CBO debt projections 2024–2034).

I. AMERICA'S DEBT RATIO BURDEN IN 2024

1   Coburn, T. (2013) *The Debt Bomb*. Thomas Nelson.

Senator Coburn's position on taxes. *Politico* article dated 12/10/2012. Poltico.com/story/2012/12/dr-no-of-senate-says-yes-to-taxes.

2   Allocation of debt among holders. *The Balance* article dated 1/1/2023. www.thebalancemoney.com/who-owns-the-us-national-debt.

The deficit for the fiscal year 2023 was $2 trillion. Article by William McBride published by the Tax Foundation on 10/12/23. https//taxfoundation.org/blog/federal-budget-deficit-2023/#.

3   Rating agency downgrades. https./budgethouse.gov/resources/staff-working-papers/us-debt-credit-rating. Reuters. www.reuters.com/markets-rates-bonds-bank-of-america.

Interest paid to foreign investors. *Washington Post* article by Jeff Stein 10/20/23.

4–5   *The International Monetary Fund recently....* As reported in the *Economist,* article, *The Debt Trap,* 6/03/2023

The conservative think tank, (G-Cato Institute quote on national debt).

The World Bank Group recently.... World Bank Group Policy Research Paper—"Finding the Tipping Point—When Sovereign Debt Turns Bad." (G-World Bank Group Study on national debt ratios.)

6–7   *The President's Budget ...* President's Budget/OMB. Table S-10 (G- President's 2025 budget).

In 2024 the World Population Review reported... World

Population Review— Debt to GDP Ratio by Country. 2024 (G-debt to GDP ratio by country.)

7–8   Federal Reserve Bank Study, *What Lessons Can Be Drawn from Japan's High Debt-to-GDP Ratio?* November 19, 2023. YiLi Chien, Ashley H. Stewart, www.stlouisfed.org/on-the-economy/2023/nov/what-lessons-can-be-drawn-japan's-high-debt-to-gdp-ratio.

II. ORIGINS AND HISTORY OF DEBT RATIO GROWTH

11   *If the graph would be extended ...* Table 2.1.
       For example, the debt increased substantially.... Table 7.1.
       As a corrective measure.... Revenue and Expenditure Control Act of 1968, H.R. 15414.

12   *The typical CEO ... New York Times* article by David Leonhardt dated September 5, 2017.
       Statistics in paragraph beginning *The Kennedy tax cuts....* Table 2.3.

15   Three successive paragraphs, the first of which began *Ironically the first person in government....* Bruce Bartlett article *Starve the Beast—Origins and Development of a Budgetary Metaphor*, page 6 of a summer 2007 article in the *Independent Review*, (G-bruce bartlett article on national debt in Independent Review.)

17   Reagan quote: taken from Bartlett testimony on May 17, 2023. (G-bruce bartlett testimony transcript).

18   Paragraph beginning *During President Reagan's time in office....* See Tables 1.1, and 7.1.

18–19 *By 1988 defense spending ...* Table 14.4.

19   *Conservative economist Bruce Bartlett ...* Bruce Bartlett testimony to Congress ... (G-Bruce Bartlett testimony transcript).

20   Lawrence Lindsey quote.... Bloomberg article by Justin Fox, "The Mostly Forgotten Tax Increases of 1982–1993," December 15, 2017.
       During the Reagan Administration the ratio of income tax revenues to GDP ... Table 2.3.

21   The Pledge (G-Americans for Tax Reform).

22   *True to their pledge.... Washington Post,* August 6, 1993 "Senate Passes Clinton Budget ... "

The Pledge. See web site atr.org.

*By the year 2000....*Table 7.1.

23   Paragraph immediately following graph. Tables 1.2 and 2.3. Statistics in first paragraph: Tables 1.2 and 2.3.

Statistics in paragraph beginning *The basic premise:* Tables 2.3 and 7.1.

25   William A. Niskanen Report (G-William A. Niskanen Report Starve the Beast summary).

26   *Bruce Barlett, who was also...* His book *The New American Economy* mentioned he was fired by a Republican leaning think tank. His résumé, which can be found by Googling his name, indicates he was employed at one time by the Cato Institute.

Book *The New American Economy—The Failure of Reaganomics and a New Way Forward,* Palgrave MacMillan © Bruce Bartlett 2009.

28   *In that year ...* Table 2.3.

The higher rates and the continuing recovery ... Table 2.3.

30   The Trump Years. Quotes from 2016 campaign: (G-Trump quote about King of Debt).

Truman quote: Opening page of book by Andy Borowitz, *Profiles in Ignorance. How America's Politicians Got Dumb and Dumber.* Simon & Schuster, Inc. Copyright © 2022 by Andy Borowitz.

Trump bankruptcies.... *Washington Post* article dated September 26, 2016, "Fact Check. Has Trump declared bankruptcy four or six times?"

31–32   Statistics in paragraph beginning, *With the national debt:* Tables 7.1, 1.1 and 2.3.

Most likely he was invoking Supply Side theory.... June 19 *New York Times* article titled, "Trump Awards Presidential Medal of Freedom to Arthur Laffer."

In an interview with Sean Hannity.... Reported in January 14, 2021, *ProPublica article.* www.propublica.org/article/national-debt-trump.

Statistics in paragraph beginning *We saw what happened ...* Tables 1.1 and 2.3.

33   George Will quote ... July 22, 2019, YouTube interview with Judy Woodruff.

Statistics in paragraph beginning *A comparison of fiscal results* ... Table 1.2 and Table 4.2.

34 *At a fund raiser* ... NBC news report, April 7 and other news outlets.

Niskanen Center quote ... (G-niskanen center article about starve the beasts).

34 *An article published on March 27, 2023....* (G-March 27 article by Center for American Progress).

About 80% of the spending differential ... Table 14.5.

III. THE PANDEMIC-CAUSED DEBT EXPLOSION

38 Statistics in paragraph beginning *In 2020, the Congress and President Trump....* Tables 1.1, 1.2 and 2.3.

Deficit figures in paragraph beginning *Like former President Obama, President Biden* ... Table 1.1.

39 *Income tax revenues climbed to....* Table 2.3.

The authors of the recent book ... *The Greatest Ponzi Scheme on Earth.* Distributed by Simon & Schuster, Copyright © 2024 by Leslie A. Rubin and Daniel J. Mitchell

In four of the next six years.... Table 2.3.

41 *With the Trump tax cuts continuing....* Table 2.3.

The CBO estimates that the FRA ... June 2023 report of CBO titled, "How the Fiscal Responsibility Act of 2023 Affects CBO's Projection of Federal Debt." (G-CBO projections of effect of fiscal responsibility act.)

IV. WHERE THE MONEY IS AND ISN'T

44 *Going down the wealth ladder....* (G-Federal Reserve Study on Wealth Concentration).

Not surprisingly ... January 10 article titled, "The rich now own a record share of stocks appearing in AXIOS." https://www.axios.com/2024/01/10 wealthy-own-record-share-stock-market.

Moving from wealth to income... Statista study.... (G-statista study on income concentration in europe 2023)

Of the 38 reporting OECD countries ... American

Compass study titled, "A Guide to U.S. Economic Inequality." (G-american compass study on wealth inequality).

45   *New York Times reporter Christopher Leonard.* Book Simon & Schuster Paperbacks, Copyright © 2022 by Christopher Leonard.

Statistics on agricultural subsidies were reported in the February 24, 2023 issue of the *Kansas Reflector.* (G-agricultural subsidies going to top 1%).

Paragraph beginning *Studies made by the OECD* ... OECD Data Wage Levels: (G-oecd studies on low wage jobs.)

Paragraph beginning *Governmental benefits do not lessen the gap.* International Labor Organization study (G-Countries that provide paid maternity leave.)

Paragraph beginning *Subsidized day care* ... OECD study titled, "Public spending on daycare and early childhood education" (G-oecd report early childhood spending by country.)

46   *A 2020 study by the Rand Corporation* ... Study titled, "Trends in Income From 1975–2018." (G-Rand Corporation study on income inequality).

47   *A Federal Reserve Report* ... Reported in May 23, 2023, edition of *Fortune.*

Concentration of income ... Federal Reserve Board report titled, "Distribution of Household Wealth in the U.S. since 1989." (G-federal reserve study of household wealth distribution).

Grants made pursuant to the CARES Act ... S. 3548 – 116th Congress (2019-2020) The CARES Act.

48–49   *Aid to privately owned businesses.... under the PPP forgivable loan program.* H.R. 7352—117th Congress (2021–2022).

A total of $793 billion in loans ... PPP Loan Forgiveness Fact Sheet (G-loans disbursed and forgiven under ppp loan forgiveness).

50   *They received a $4.6 million loan....* ESPN report, April 27, 2020 (G-L A Lakers ppp loan).

But a business owned by Tom Brady ... CNBC report, December 5, 2020 (G-tom brady ppp loan).

A study by the Federal Reserve Bank of St. Louis titled,

"Was the Paycheck Protection Program Effective?" (G-frb of st louis study on ppp loan forgiveness).

51   *In a report dated June* ... SBA Inspector General Report titled, "COVID-19."

52   *The airline industry received* ... U.S. Treasury publication titled, "Airline and National Security Relief Programs" (G-Cares Act aid to airlines in us).
       One airline, American Airlines.... New York Times, April 14, 2020, updated March 17, 2020.
       American Airlines stock repurchases reported in March 25, 2020, *Motley Fool* article titled, "Airlines Did Not Waste All Their Cash Flow On Share Buybacks: American Airlines Did."
       Data on warrants and 2012 share buybacks taken from AA shareholder reports in 2020.
       The terms contrast sharply ... CNBC report, December 9, 2013.

53   *In her book* ... copyright © Carol Roth, first published June 29, 2021, HarperCollins Broadside Books.
       John Miltimore article ... Foundation for Economic Education. (G-jon miltimore article July 8, 2022, on Federal Reserve.)

V. OBSTACLES

57   *The Blue Dog Democrats* ... See *Washington Post* article dated August 8, 2023, "Dwindling Blue Dog Democrats Seek to State a Comeback for Moderates."
       Two paragraphs concerning the Pledge ... See *Roll Call* article titled, "Tax pledge's father bestows blessing on GOP debt limit package" by Paul Krawzak.

58   Quote from Bruce Bartlett book. See third note for page 26.

61   *In 1790, approximately 90% of the labor force* ... Quora (G-what percentage of the population lived on farms in the 1899s?)

61   *President Biden's long-term fiscal plan* ... President's Budget/OMB (G-president's 2025 budget.
       But deficits over that period ... Table S-10 of the budget
       The GOP controlled Congress.... Roll Call article dated

September 19, 2023, titled, "Balanced-budget plan un-veiled by House Republicans." (G-Republican deficit re-duction plan)

63   Paragraph beginning *According to the Center for Budget and Policy Priorities* ... Report dated March 24, 2023, titled, "House Republicans Pledge to Cut Appropriated Programs to 2022 Level ..." (G-republican deficit reduc-tion plan).

Infrastructure spending statistics.... *Statista* study titled, "global investment on inland transport infrastructure as share of GDP in 2021, by selected countries." (G-infra-structure spending by country).

65   Karen Dynan quote. Reported in *New York Times* Sub-scriber Only Newsletter dated January 8, 2024, written by Peter Coy.

65   *According to the CBO...* CBO publication "The Budget and Economic Outlook 2024 to 2034 (G-CBO deficit projections).

VI. STEP 1: REDUCE THE DEBT

69   Discussion of Domenici-Rivlin Task Force ... Biparti-san Policy Center publication titled, "Domenici-Rivlin Debt Reduction Task Force Plan 2.0" (G-Domenici-Rivlin reporter).

71   *But as bonds mature* ... Rates based on treasury data, early May 2024.

The top 1% have ... Federal Reserve Bank of St. Louis report dated March 22, 2024 (G-top 1% of total wealth).

In early May 2024 ... *New York Times* May 3, 2024, guest essay, "It's Time to Tax the Billionaires" by Gabriel Zuc-man. Taxes refer to all taxes, not just income tax.

74   *Just such a proposal was made ... by Donald Trump ...* *VOX* article dated January 31, 2019, titled, "That time Donald Trump proposed a 14.5% wealth tax" (G-wealth tax proposed by Donald Trump).

Data in paragraph beginning *With a few exceptions* ... Tax Foundation/Europe report dated February 27, 2024, titled, "Wealth Taxes in Europe-2024," by Cristina Enache (G-wealth taxes in Europe).

76 *The Federal Reserve Board....* Federal Reserve Board report titled, "Distribution of Household Wealth in the U.S. Since 1989," (G-federal reserve study on wealth concentration).

78 *Recently a group of at least* ... DW January 8, 2024, article by Thomas Latschan titled, "Davos: When will you tax extreme wealth? Super rich ask." G-letter from 260 wealthy persons asking for tax increase).

Since the 2017 tax cuts ... Numerous articles and news reports accessible under (G-stock buybacks since trump tax cuts).

VII. STEP 2: REVERSE THE DEBT RATIO TRAJECTORY

82 Statistics in paragraph beginning *In comparison with other developed countries* ... OECD Data, Tax revenue (G-OECD taxes by country).

83 *The U.S. ranks 32nd* ... OECD Family Database—Public spending on early childhood education. (G-oecd report early childhood education spending by country).

The U.S. has a much higher poverty rate ... First Focus on Children study dated November 7, 2022, titled, "Keeping up with progress: how the U.S. can follow the world's lead on child poverty" reporting that due to the Child Tax Credit law the U.S. improved from the 31st highest child poverty rate among 34 countries in the study to 24th. Child poverty is disproportionately higher among children of color. The tax credit has since expired. (G-child poverty rate in the U.S. compared to other countries.)

85 *Rates range from....* World Population Review study titled, "VAT tax by Country 2024" (G-VAT tax rates by country).

Countries & People. (G-happiest country in the world.)

87 *Some conservative analysts and organizations* ... Heritage Foundation publication dated March 3, 2023, titled, "In 1 Chart, How Much the Rich Pay in Taxes." (G-Heritage Foundation Tax Policy).

Income and tax data taken from March 13, 2024, publication by the Tax Foundation titled, "Summary of the Latest Federal Income Tax Data, 2024 Update" https://taxfoundation.org/data//all/federal/latest-federal-income-tax-data.

88   *In 1928, those with incomes* ... CATO Institute study, winter of 2021, titled, "The Economic Impact of Tax Chages, 1920-1939" (G-percent of all taxes paid by wealthy in 1928 to present).

That would be the equivalent of.... Computation by *Amortization.org* (G-What is $100 in 1960 worth in 2024?)

VIII. AGING POPULATION CHALLENGE

90   *Nearly one out of every five...*. Pew Research study dated December 20, 2010, titled, "Baby Boomers Approach 65-Glumly" (G-what percentage of the population will be baby boomers in 2030).

Although the U.S. has fallen behind ... Peterson KFF Health System Tracker study dated January 30, 2024, titled, "How does U.S. life expectancy compare to other countries?" (G-U.S. life expectancy compared to other countries).

First paragraph under heading "Social Security" See Concord Coalition study titled, "History and Future of the Social Security Trust Fund, Parts I, II and III." (G-concord coalition history social security trust fund).

91   *Annual surpluses* ... Social Security Administration Trust Fund Data. https://www.ssa.gov/oact/STATS/table4a3.html.

By law, all moneys in the Social Security Trust Fund ... Social Security Administration publication titled, "Trust fund FAQs" (G-how is social security trust fund invested?)

In 1999, a commentary by Robert D. Reischauer ... (G-robert Reischauer article on social security trust fund).

The value of stocks in the S&P 500 ... Macrotrends chart titled, SPDR S&P 500 ETF—31 Year Stock Price history/ SPY. (The SPDR ETF is constructed to match the performance of the S&P 500.) (G-spdr historical prices).

94   *A Republican study...*. RSC Budget FY 202. Preserving American Freedom (G-republican study group 2020 budget bill).

The amount that the U.S. spends ... Peterson KDF study titled, "How does health care spending in the U.S.

compare with other countries?" (G-health care spending by country).

95 Health care administrative costs quoted were derived from a study by CAP 20 titled, "Excess administrative costs burden the U.S. health care system." (G-medicare administrative costs compared to private insurance).

Fortunately, the number of uninsured.... Peter G. Peterson Foundation Study dated November 19, 2023, titled, "The share of Americans without health insurance in 2022 reached a record low" (G-what percent of the us population does not have health insurance?)

IX. GROWING THE ECONOMY THROUGH IMMIGRATION REFORM

97 Statistics in paragraph beginning *Robust economic growth will require* ... Immigration Learning Center study titled, "Quick Immigration Statistics: United States."

POST-ELECTION ADDENDUM

Never let yourself be persuaded that any Great Man, any one leader, is necessary for the salvation of America. When America consists of one leader and 158 million followers, it will no longer be America.
Dwight D. Eisenhower, statement made
when population of U.S. was 158 million

This book was originally completed and published before the elections held in November 2024. During the presidential campaign, the threat to our economy posed by America's increasing Debt Ratio was hardly mentioned, let alone addressed by either candidate in a plan. To the contrary, both candidates proposed tax cuts that would increase the Debt Ratio even further. The election was won by the candidate whose proposals, according to the Committee for a Responsible Federal Budget (CRFB), would result in the greater increase in the national debt.

The previous pages refer to a national debt of $34 trillion. As the year 2024 drew to a close, the debt had surpassed $36 trillion ($36,000,000,000,000). Yes, that's twelve zeroes. In June 2024, the CBO projected that by 2034, the national debt held by the public would grow to $50.7 trillion, a record 122% of GDP. (Total debt would be more.) Since the projection was based on existing law, the CBO's projection assumed that individual and certain other tax rate reductions enacted in 2017 would be allowed to expire at the end of 2025, as scheduled. If the tax cuts are extended, the CBO projected that by 2034, the publicly held debt would increase by an additional $4.6 trillion.

President Trump advocates extension of the 2017 tax cuts, as well as additional cuts. Altogether, according to the CRFB, Trump's economic plan would add $7.75 trillion to the previous estimate, increasing the projected publicly held debt in 2034 to more than $58 trillion. This would almost certainly result in an interest burden of more than $2 trillion per year.

The confirmation of hedge fund manager Scott Bessent as secretary of the treasury offers some hope, as he at least recognizes the danger our growing national debt poses to our economy. He suggests what he calls a "3/3/3" deficit reduction plan. The first "3" represents his goal of reducing the deficit to 3% of GDP by 2028. This is an admirable goal, which, absent a recession or other extraordinary adverse event, would reverse the Debt Ratio.

Mr. Bessent's second "3" represents 3% GDP growth. (He must be referring to real GDP growth as opposed to constant dollar growth which, due to inflation, is typically higher.) In fiscal 2024, real growth was 2.8%, but the treasury still had a deficit of around $1.9 trillion. With GDP in the range of $29 trillion, an additional 0.2% of real growth would add about

$58 billion, a large sum, but not a major improvement when measured against debt in the trillions of dollars. Like Mr. Bessent's first "3," the second "3" is an admirable goal but is not a plan.

Mr. Bessent's final "3" represents increasing the daily production of oil in the U.S. from the current 13 million barrels to 16 million. At $70 per barrel, this would add nearly $76 billion to GDP each year. This assumes that production can be increased by the amount he suggests and that the additional production does not depress the price of oil. Setting aside the political question of whether we should be increasing oil production, the additional GDP and revenue realized from the increased production would represent only a small fraction of what is needed. Whether production is increased also depends on the price of oil being maintained at a sufficient level for oil companies to make a profit. The decision to increase drilling rests with the oil companies, not the government.

Mr. Bessent's concern about the debt has not prevented him from expressing support for extending the 2017 tax cuts. Consequently, with a treasury secretary supporting extension and a Republican Congress largely beholden to President Trump, extension of the 2017 tax cuts is practically a foregone conclusion. The debate will likely center around how many of Trump's additional proposed tax cuts will be passed, what tariffs to adopt, and what spending reductions will be enacted to slow the growth of red ink.

President Trump has appointed Elon Musk to chair a new department, called the Department of

Governmental Efficiency (DOGE). Mr. Musk has stated that he believes government spending can be reduced by $2 trillion annually, nearly one third of the federal budget.

Savings of anywhere close to $2 trillion could not be realized solely from increased efficiency in delivery of existing government services. The government could eliminate 100% of discretionary spending other than defense and veterans' benefits and still not save even $1 trillion, much less $2 trillion.

Vivek Ramaswamy, an American entrepreneur who was to serve as co-chair of DOGE until withdrawing, suggested going through government departments and eliminating half the employees by firing those with Social Security numbers beginning with an odd number. But the total payroll of all departments of government is just over $300 billion, so the savings in reducing payroll by half would only be about $150 billion. But even that amount of savings could be illusory. To continue to offer the same level of service with one half the payroll, the government would need to employ outside contractors. Some departments, such as the FAA, are already short of staff. Reducing the number of air traffic controllers would be a serious blow to air safety.

Mr. Musk has advocated elimination of the Department of Education (DOE). In fiscal 2024, that department managed about $241 billion in federal spending, which included administrative costs of about 3%. The largest components were student aid, about $170 billion; grants in support of elementary and secondary education, $27 billion; and grants for special education, $20 billion.

The aid to elementary and secondary education is disproportionately directed toward schools with a high percentage of students whose family incomes are at or below the poverty level. Those schools also tend to have higher percentages of students with special needs than other schools. I am familiar with an elementary public charter school in Kansas City, Missouri, that serves the urban poor, predominantly minority students. This school receives about 15% of its annual budget from federal grants. The balance comes from state funding and private donations. The funding from the DOE is vital to meeting the needs of children who, in addition to living in poverty, have often experienced trauma from the effect of gun violence impacting their families and neighborhoods. The additional funding helps this school offer an enriched program, including pre-kindergarten and a lower student/teacher ratio than other schools. Losing federal aid would be a severe blow to this school's program. Undoubtedly there are other schools across the country in a similar situation.

One wonders if Mr. Musk contends that the U.S. is spending too much on education, or if he expects the states to replace this funding through higher taxes. States that would be most affected are largely solid red states. Fifteen of the 18 states receiving the most per-student aid for elementary education are reliably Republican. Many of those states also provide less-than-average support per student in public schools. Some, like my state of Kansas and neighboring Missouri, are among the most resistant to enacting tax increases.

Eliminating federal student aid for college students would likely result in the loss of all or most of the current $170 billion in student aid that the DOE provides. With many students choosing to attend a college outside of their home state, the problem of administering student aid at the state level would become quite complex. If a student from one state wants to attend college in another state, which state would provide student aid? Quite likely, neither. There is also no assurance that states would pick up the slack even for students who attend college in their own states.

Another department that is possibly targeted for elimination is the Consumer Finance Protection Bureau. Depending on one's political leanings, that department could be a candidate for elimination. But the savings would be less than $1 billion annually. Let's put it another way: If the goal is to cut spending by $2 trillion, elimination of this department would save less than one two thousandths of the amount needed.

The government spending which should be given the highest priority for reduction is interest cost, now running close to $1 trillion per year. The treasury pays more than $200 billion in interest to foreign governments and investors each year. This is five times the amount of humanitarian aid budgeted for the U.S. Agency for International Development.

The only sure way to reduce interest cost is to reduce the debt. As previously suggested, debt reduction could be achieved through a temporary wealth tax or surtax on wealthier individuals. The current generation has reaped the benefits of sacrifices made by previous generations. Are we so special that we cannot sacrifice to help create a better future for those who come after? Reducing the debt through a temporary deficit reduction tax plan might be considered a sacrifice, but it would not impair the standard of living of those of us who would be asked to bear the cost. Reduction in the debt could also benefit the current economy by bringing down interest rates. We should get on with it.

The previous pages highlighted the vast disparity in wealth and income between the wealthiest Americans and virtually everyone else that existed in 2024. Now, in early 2025, the gap has grown larger. Bloomberg reports that the value of publicly traded stocks increased by $11 trillion in 2024. With the wealthiest 10% of Americans holding 93% of publicly traded stocks, and a very high percentage of that number being held by the top 1%, the additional wealth created by increased stock market values accrued mainly to the wealthiest Americans. The need and feasibility of the deficit reduction pay-down suggested in the previous pages have become even more obvious. Lawmakers just need the necessary political will to take decisive action.

Mr. Musk has stated that the government must live within its means. But as pointed out in previous chapters, a major reason why the government does not now have the means has been tax cuts. The wealthiest 1%

have far more combined wealth than the national debt, and several times the combined wealth of the bottom 50%. As Warren Buffet stated in 2006, *"There's class warfare, all right, but it's my class, the rich class, that's making war, and we're winning."* According to statistics published by the Federal Reserve Board, the wealth disparity trend from 2006 to the end of 2024 has continued unabated.

On the surface, the election of Donald Trump to a second term is another win for that wealthy class, but if the growth in the Debt Ratio is not reversed, there will be no winners. We will all be losers, as paying interest on the national debt becomes so burdensome that, as predicted by Senator Coburn, the only way out is hyperinflation. Loss of the dollar as the world's reserve currency would be all but assured.

Economists agree that growth in the treasury's debt has a material effect on interest rates. Concerns about likely additional deficit-financed tax cuts under a Trump administration have been a major contributor to higher long-term rates. From late September 2024 to the end of January 2025, the yield on 10-year treasuries increased by 70 basis points (0.7%).

Because of the government's massive debt, changes in interest rates have an outsized effect on the Treasury's interest burden. An increase of 0.7% in the effective interest rate paid on the total national debt would increase interest expense by more than $200 billion annually. The 10-year treasury rate not only impacts the amount of interest the government must pay but is also a factor in setting other interest rates, including home loans.

So, what can voters do? As futile as the effort might appear to be, voters need to insist that the first order of business for Congress is adopting a responsible fiscal plan, preferably bipartisan. This should be done before the 2017 tax cuts are extended and before any further tax cuts are enacted. Voters can wish President Trump and Mr. Musk well in their efforts to reduce spending in a responsible way, but we do not know which spending reductions will be approved by Congress. We also do not know which tariffs will be put in place or what effect they will have on revenues. Until Congress has a better idea of the impact of those proposals, it is irresponsible to extend the Trump tax cuts or adopt new tax reductions.

This Addendum would not be complete without mentioning President Trump's suggestion that revenues from tariffs replace the income tax. One wonders if he is aware that in 2024 imports of goods and income tax revenues were each about $3 trillion. Implementation of this suggestion would require tariffs to average an impossible 100%. President Trump's previous business experience of multiple bankruptcies, his statements about renegotiating the national debt (see page 30), his tax cuts that have been a major contributor to the growth in debt, and his proposal to have tariffs replace the income tax demonstrate that his judgment on fiscal matters cannot be trusted. Congress must take the lead.

Adopting a realistic plan to reverse the Debt Ratio

will depend on the extent to which members of Congress are willing to exercise their own independent judgment. Donald Trump has been elected president, not emperor. Members of Congress must place their responsibility to restore fiscal sanity above their loyalty to the president or any pledge to Mr. Norquist. As voters, we must make sure that lawmakers know they will be held accountable if they fail to do so.

About the Author

Howard Mick worked fifty-two years in the legal field, retiring twelve years ago. After serving as an Army reservist, he joined a leading Kansas City law firm in 1959, where he specialized in business law, including public stock offerings, mergers and acquisitions, and bank regulation. His work, particularly in the banking sector, earned him recognition in *Best Lawyers in America*.

For over forty years, Howard has been concerned about America's fiscal policies and the growing national debt. On multiple occasions, he expressed these views through letters to the editor of the *Kansas City Star*. To communicate his insights more effectively, he decided to write a book that explores the overlooked aspects of fiscal policy in recent decades.

Howard believes that voters today need a clear understanding of how these policies have shaped the national debt and wealth distribution. Drawing on his extensive legal experience, Howard aims to provide readers with the crucial knowledge needed to navigate and influence the future of America's fiscal landscape.